Walking Tour Guiding
The Ultimate Handbook

Dawn A Denton

Copyright © 2021 Dawn A Denton

All rights reserved.

ISBN 978-0-9926820-8-8

DEDICATION

To my dearest Contiki family:

Thank you for filling my heart with love and laughter,

my memories with adventure

and my life with friendships.

CONTENTS

Section 1: Introduction

1	About	1
2	What is a Walking Tour?	5
3	The Walking Tour Experience	9
4	Aspiration & Inspiration	12

Section 2: You the Guide

5	Skills & Qualities of a Guide	16
6	Knowledge	19
7	What a Guide Could Know & Share	22
8	Personality	24
9	Your Appearance for Confidence	26
10	Nervousness	28
11	Controlling Your Nerves	30
12	Involve Your Guests	33
13	Humour	36

Section 3: Presenting

14	Body Language	38
15	Using Your Hands	40
16	Know Your Voice	41
17	How to be Heard	45
18	Barriers to Communication	47
19	Effective Communication	51
20	Communicating with Your Guests	53
21	Assess Your Delivery	56

Section 4: Your Group

22	Visitor Expectations	59
23	Group Management	62
24	Answering Questions	65
25	Difficult Questions	69

Section 5: Your Walking Tour

26	Your Primary Subject	71
27	Add to Your Jigsaw	73
28	Five Senses	75
29	Colour Your Walks	78
30	Storytelling	81
31	Safe Environment	83
32	Create Your Walking Tour	84

Section 6: Questions & Answers

33	Between Stops	89
34	Drying Up	91
35	Common Mistakes	94
36	When People Leave	96
37	Meeting Your Guests	97
38	What Questions Tell Us	99

Section 7: Professional Tips

39	Tools of the Trade	100
40	Bodies & Organisations	102
41	Talking to the Public	106
42	From the Professionals	113
43	That's a Wrap	116
	About the Author	117

ACKNOWLEDGMENTS

A huge thank you to the late Katrine Prince for her inspiration. I thoroughly enjoyed the few classes I had with her after she so sadly got sick, and I have treasured the notes I took while learning from her.

My Contiki 'family' has played a huge role in my continued love and passion for guiding. *So many of you inspire me daily. I truly value our adventures together and our continued friendships, wherever you are in the world.*

With Dan Wood, my darling 'other half' (whom I met while guiding), I share a love of the profession, which has given us hours of discussions and debates over a few bottles of whiskey. *Your experience and expertise have been invaluable in completing this book and my training programmes.*

The Content College community have cheered me on at every step. *Your encouragement has meant this book did not take another 20 years to write. Thank you!*

Willem van der Walt, writer, and my uncle – he has always been my 'go to' person when I write. *I hope my DNA has even just a small bit of your talent and creativity*

Sandy Barker – when we met on Contiki training all those years ago, who would have thought we would both be published writers and still friend across the seas. *Your career as a writer has been so admirable and a true inspiration.*

Lynette Gonga of Adventure Horizons Africa (Zimbabwe) asked for my help to train more guides. *Thank you for reaching out, Lynette, or this book would never have happened.*

And thank you to YOU, dear reader. I hope you find some nuggets between the pages to take into your walking tour guiding, whether you choose it as a career or a hobby.

Walking tour guiding will bring you much joy!

Section 1: Introduction

CHAPTER 1: ABOUT

Welcome to the exciting world of walking tour guiding!

You have a passion for your village, town, city, suburb or region, or you have a love of something unique, which you would love to share with others.
In this book, I will teach you all I know to arm you with the knowledge and skills to design and craft walking tours. You are multi-talented, so you can use this information (the basic theory behind guiding) to create something special in whatever niche you find your passion.
I hope you will find inspiration and some gems that will work for you to lead and create something special.
This is going to be fun, and I look forward to sharing this journey with you.

About Me

I boarded a plane for London, United Kingdom, in Johannesburg, South Africa in 1995 with a backpack, boyfriend and a teaching qualification. The teaching was tough, the boyfriend was useless, but the backpack gave me many new opportunities.
I saw an advertisement in a magazine for travellers:
"Do you love travel?"
At that point in my life, I had only been out of South Africa to Zimbabwe, Botswana, and the United States. I thought:
"I am sure I would love it, if I did travel."
And so, my guiding career as a tour manager / director started with Contiki Holidays. I took tour groups around Europe for 10 seasons: lunching in Paris, partying in Florence, rafting in

the Tyrol. From concerts to coffee, and champagne to chocolate, to shopping and shows. I made lifelong friends, who are now 'family'. I experienced the ups and downs of guiding, but most importantly, I fell in love with walking tours. While on my feet, exploring, I found the soul of guiding. I decided to put my toothbrush down for more than two days at a time. I got to work at (and then manage) the Contiki Customer Service / Departure Centre in London. But, I had 'itchy feet' and so I trained as a London City Green Badge Guide to lead walking tours in the heart of London – the Square Mile. And I worked on my days off taking day trips from London to Dover, Leeds Castle, Bath and Stonehenge. I returned to the classroom and taught Travel and Tourism at A-Level but guiding called me back. After volunteering at the London Olympics in 2012, l joined Trafalgar Tours to take tour groups around the United Kingdom and Ireland, and Australian Pacific Touring took me to Europe, the Balkans and Russia.

Why I wrote this book

When I moved out of London, I found myself in a lively, innovative, and forward-thinking Somerset town. I was instantly engaged – networking events, speaking opportunities, and business growth groups.
I was employed by the town council to teach a group of enthusiasts how to guide. The council's aim is to engage those who live here and who are passing through to explore the wonderful history and stories that make our town so special.
I created resources for the training, which became an online course on a global platform. Through this course, I was contacted by a lady in Zimbabwe who needed my help. She wanted to train more guides in Zimbabwe. But internet is not widely accessible and mobile data is expensive, so an online course was not an option. A book was the best opportunity for her to reach more people and train more guides to lead walking tours in Zimbabwe.
So, here it is…

I have been looking forward to getting this book into your hands for many years. I am so pleased to have you here!

This book is divided into 7 sections:

1. What is guiding?
2. You the guide: what you say (your content)
3. Presenting: how you say it (skills and communication)
4. The Group: why you say it (what they want to see and hear)
5. Create your Walking Tour
6. Questions & Answers
7. From the Professionals

By the end of this book, you should understand the following:

- The skills needed to lead a walking tour.
- What goes into making a good walking tour.
- Guiding and communication skills.
- How to handle visitors and take good care of them.
- Tourism opportunities in and around the town of the area where you are guiding.

You will not learn how to lead a walking tour from *only* reading a book. You need to practise and go out and DO!
At the end of every section, you will find an activity. These questions and tasks will form the foundation of your walks and give you a wider understanding of your role as a walking tour guide.
Walking tours are about the place and the audience.

Your tours are not about you!
Guides do far more than educate their guests. So, go out there to *inform AND charm*!

Activity

Record your goals as a walking tour guide at the start of your journey:
- Why do you want to lead walking tours?
- What do you hope to achieve as a walking tour guide?
- Where would you like to guide?
- Do you have different walking tours in mind?

Keep these answers safe so that you can look at them again at the end of the book.

CHAPTER 2:
WHAT IS A WALKING TOUR?

1. The Tourism Industry

Tourism is an exciting industry and, of course, it is extremely competitive. Countries, counties, towns, and regions around the world compete to attract tourists. They all aim to deliver a superior tourist experience to ensure repeat business, referrals, and funding opportunities. And of course, have a positive impact on all areas of the community.

Thus, the value of walking tour guiding may seem small, but it is essential to an overall tourism plan and product.

2. What is a Walking Tour?

According to the World Federation of Tourist Guiding Associations:

"A Tourist Guide is a person who… interprets the cultural and natural heritage of an area."

There are three parts to a walking tour:
- What the guide says – content
- How the guide says it – delivery / presentation
- Who the guide is saying it to – the group

Guiding is an art. When people spend time with a good walking tour guide, they are drawn to the place, engaged with the stories and develop a fondness for their guide.

Tour guides can be employed to work full time or part-time for companies such as tour operators, wildlife parks, amusement parks, museums, historic sites, cruise ships, local town councils and more.

There are many volunteering opportunities available too, or guides can be self-employed.

On their Feet

A walking tour is NOT an outside lecture. That is especially important! It is about visitors being on their feet, between the locals.

Guests get to feel the vibe, smell the town, hear the chatter and the accents. They get to experience the atmosphere. It is an intimate opportunity for them to speak with someone who knows more about the town than they do and immerse themselves in a community.

Nooks and crannies get explored. It is thus the guide's job to let the site speak, tell the local tales, and shares its secrets. Because it is a deeply personal experience that means so much more than taking home a souvenir.

Ambassador / Representative

The guides are the gatekeepers who showcase the site. They are thus armed with historic, geographic, architectural, religious, industrial, cultural, social and natural history of the area.

Importantly, guides build trust so that visitors rely on their local information. They are in an unique position to advise their guest about places to eat, rest, stay, and what activities and events are on in the area. Thus, guides open the doors to our visitors so they can spend money in the local economy and are a vital advertisement for the community.

Role of the Guide

The primary role of the guide is to look after, and enthusiastically, provide information that the tourist or visitors can use to enhance their experience.

Remember, tour guiding marries the place and the audience, with your guests. It is not about the tour guide. With experience, a guide can give the guests as much of a 'live like a local' experience as possible.

A guide gives the gift of words and creativity to 'build' landscapes, tell stories, reveal the secrets of history, and create memorable experiences. They aim to have their guests leave the walking tour with some knowledge, but most importantly having created new memories and experiences.

A guide may have small groups, but an emphasis on big personalisation will enhance the experience for everyone!

And that is exciting!

3. Why Do People Go on a Walking Tour?
- *To learn something new:* Your guests may be new to the area; they may want to learn more about where they live, or they are passing through.
- *To understand what they are looking at:* People may have asked themselves about something for years and have just never found out.
- *To immerse themselves in everything local:* being amongst the people gives a visitor a true sense of the community.
- *To enjoy themselves:* A walking tour should always be an experience the guests will treasure and remember for years to come.
- *Personal care and attention:* This might be subconscious, but people may come on a walking tour because they want something special. They want to feel like they are getting something others are not getting or experiencing. It is important to remember that every person on the tour needs that special personal care and attention. Obviously, this personal attention is within reason because you may have a group of to 50 people and it would be impossible in a short space of time to give everyone personal attention, but it is possible to make them all feel special in other ways. We all want to feel a bit special, don't we?

It is so easy to forget why your guests are there. For some people, you are fulfilling a life dream by showing them new things and places, or they may have saved up a long time to be with you.

Activity

This activity will give you a starting point to build your walking tours.

From your own experience of walking tour guides, write down some thoughts around the following:

- What do visitors expect of a good tour guide?
- What are the key roles and responsibilities of an effective tour guide?
- What preparations are needed before taking out a walking tour?
- How does a tour guide handle questions (especially from difficult guests)?
- What are the qualities of a good tour guide?

Being conscious of why THEY are there, helps you to be more aware of why YOU are there.

This will have an impact on the expectations your guests have, as well as the expectations you place on yourself.

CHAPTER 3:
THE WALKING TOUR EXPERIENCE

Katrine Prince was a lecturer on my City of London guiding course. She qualified as a London registered Blue Badge Tourist Guide in 1974. In 1984 she took over as Director of Studies at the London Tourist Board and in the 1990s she became involved in the Federation of Tourist Guide Associations in Europe. She was the founder trustee of the Institute of Tourist Guiding in 2002, and was about to become president, at the time of her untimely death in 2004.

She was a great inspiration to me and my guiding, and this story, by Katrine, is what walking tours are all about.

The Story of Shula

"What an attractive person", I thought as I watched a young girl approach our small group gathered in the Town Square for a walking tour. As she drew closer, her dress, simple but spruce, her face broke into a warm smile and she removed her dark glasses as she spoke.

"Good morning! You must be waiting to join me in discovering the small town of ours"

Introducing herself as Shula, she asked where we were all from, how long we had been on the island and how long we were staying. The tour would last about an hour and a half, and we would finish where we were starting the tour, in the town square.

"Please be careful crossing our narrow roads. Although we have few motorcars, the cyclists can be quite threatening. And a reminder that we drive on the right-hand side of the road."

Drawing a small boy to the front of the group, and checked that the Japanese lady at the back understood her English, Shula pointed out the star-shaped fountain in the centre of the square, and explained how it symbolized the recent history of the island.

"We will slip down that passageway, between the cafe and the paper shop," she mentioned as many of us stopped briefly to take a photograph of the fountain.

Walking Tour Guiding

I caught up with the group as I had lost them from view. They had reached the end of the passageway and were emerging into a large internal courtyard shaded by an umbrella shaped tree.

"Let's go and stand in the shade of the tree out of the sun. I would like to tell you about the pale blue house opposite with a small wrought-iron balcony."

In fact, several houses were pale blue, but only one had a balcony.

We positioned ourselves in the welcoming shade so we could see both the house in question, and Shula herself. We learnt of the general development of the town as she pointed out the architectural influences and the peculiarities that had come about locally. Since the mayor's office was in the square, we also learned about local government structure and how the town's inhabitants lived.

And so, the walk continued. We crossed the small river that ran through the town centre, and we noticed a strange object bobbing about in the water. Shula drew our attention to it and told us that the object was in fact tethered to the river base and was a container for a water pollution measure.

In the busier main street, Shula wanted us to have a good view of the local synagogue and be able to hear her too. She shepherded us against the wall of a house so that her voice reached us clearly. She spoke more slowly, and the wall acted as a soundboard for those of us at the back of the group.

An hour and a half later we found ourselves back in the square, where we had started the tour.

We thanked Shula and went off together to the cafe for a relaxing drink.

As I remarked to two of my newfound friends a week later, Shula had succeeded not only in giving us the information we had sought but had opened our eyes to several aspects of the island that had not even occurred to us. What is more, she had bonded us in such a short a time into a small group that had continued to enjoy the island together, and for one of whom indeed the friendship might continue after the holiday.

Tell me. I forget.
Show me. I may remember.
Involve me and I will understand.

Katine Prince: The Art of Guiding (The Institute of Tourist Guiding; 2nd edition - 1 Oct. 2008)

Activity
- Read the 'Story of Shula' again
- Make some notes of the things you think Shula did well.

We will break it down in the next chapter.

I hope you find some inspiration in Katrine's story. It is such a great piece to reflect on, so use this 'experience' with Shula as a prompt.

CHAPTER 4:
ASPIRATION AND INSPIRATION

Shula is an example of a walking tour guide we all aspire to be. Let us have a look at how she ran her walking tour, the content she included and delivered, as well as how she managed the group.

Here goes....

- **Shula was neatly and appropriately dressed.**

She is, of course, representing her community.

- **The tour started in the Town Square.**

It is a main and central place that people can easily find.

- **Shula greeted all those waiting, with a warm, inviting smile.**

This helps guests feel at ease and know they are going to love the walking tour.

- **She confirmed that she was there for the walking tour at that time.**

It is easy for people to join the wrong tour if the guide does not confirm this at the start.

- **When she removed her sunglasses, everyone could see her eyes.**

This shows confidence. Sometimes a guide might not feel confidence, but it does not help to hide behind sunglasses. People feel at ease when they can see the eyes of the guide. Eye contact also increases engagement.

- **Shula introduced herself.**

When people know the guide's name, they can ask questions with some ease. They might also have been told to meet the guide, by name, so this gives them reassurance that they are in the right place.

- **She asked where everyone is from.**

This helps break the ice and creates a sense of unity and commonality.

- **Shula asked how long the guests were in town.**

This information helps a guide to tailor the tour. When people are just passing through, they do not need ideas for things to do after the walk – maybe only for their future visit. But if they are there for longer, the guide can recommend activities, restaurants, pubs etc.

- **Shula told them how long the walk will be and where it will end.**

This is important for people to know what to expect. When a guide lets people know where they will be ending their tour, they can also feel reassured they will not get lost. Remember, they may be unfamiliar with the town or region.

- **Shula mentioned the health and safety about crossing roads in a light-hearted way.**

This is vital. The guide does not want to scare people, but they need to be alerted to some dangers. They will be focusing on what the guide is telling them, and may not watch the traffic on the road, for example. And, of course, the surroundings are unfamiliar to them, too.

- **She got the small boy to the front.**

A good guide is aware of everyone in the group and ensures they all feel included.

- **Shula checked that everyone could hear and understand her.**

If people in the group cannot hear the guide, they may drop out along the way, which would be a real shame.

- **Shula pointed out what they could see from where they were standing.**

Preparation for a walk is important to identify things that may not be obvious the first time around, may be different from the last walk, or may seem obvious or second nature to the guide.

- **She told the group where they were going next.**

If someone stops to take a photograph, they may lose the group. This information will help them catch up.

- **She stood the group in the shade.**

Standing in the sun (or even the wind) can be uncomfortable for the group and they will not focus on the guide or the information.

- **She had a clear view of what she wanted to point out.**

She mentioned the colour of the building she was talking about, and the balcony. A common mistake is when a guide talks about something the group cannot see clearly. They lose interest and the impact of the story.

- **Shula also made sure everyone could see her.**

This is not only for reassurance, but also for those who might struggle to hear, or who do not speak the language fluently. For them, being able to see their guide, means they are more likely to hear and understand what is being said.

- **She explained exactly what she wanted everyone to look at.**

It seems simple, but guides want to avoid questions such as: "Where?" or "What are we meant to me looking at?"

- **She told them only about what they could see.**

Often guides either talk too much about what they cannot see, or miss the most obvious things, right in front of them.

- **Shula spoke about peculiarities of the town.**

People love these stories - this is what they are most likely to remember.

- **She mentioned local government.**

Guests like to know how things work in relation to their local government. Visitors are always fascinated to hear how the people live in the community.

- **When someone noticed something, she stopped to address it.**

This involves the guests, and keeps them engaged for the full experience. But of course, this must be handled within reason.

- **She used the walls as a soundboard to bounce her voice.**

When a group cannot hear the guide, they get frustrated and may leave the tour. And it protects the guide's voice – the most

valuable tool for the job.
- **Shula spoke clearly and slowly.**

There may be people who struggle to hear, or who do not speak the language well. And of course, the guide may have an accent that is unfamiliar to the group. Slowing down, also calms the guide's nerves and helps them recall the information they want to share.

- **She finished the tour in the time expected and where she said she would.**

This can be a cause of anxiety for people, especially if they are in an unfamiliar town.

- **Shula thanked everyone for coming.**

This is always a lovely and professional way to end a tour. It is also a good idea if the guide asked if there is anything they can help them with, and direct them to where they can get more information if they need it.

Why was Shula's walking tour so good?

Shula was an engaging guide who gave her guests valuable, interesting, and relevant information. She introduced her guest to new and interesting aspects of her town, not presuming they know (or did not know anything). She managed to build trust and because the group was involved in her walk, the guests bonded with each other. This is a special skill that will make your walks even more enjoyable, in the shortest time.

Overall, Shula seemed to do the job with little effort.

Activity

- Compare your notes from the previous chapter.
- Using the list above, make a note of what you do easily and naturally.
- What do you consciously need to work on?

You may want to ask those around you to help, as we are not always aware of our own strengths and weaknesses.

Section 2: You the Guide

CHAPTER 5:
SKILLS AND QUALITIES OF A GUIDE

Learning to be a brilliant guide takes hard work. And with every walking tour, you will gain more experience and you will improve.

A guide's professionalism needs to start before the walking tour begins. Make sure you consider all areas of planning, organising, coordination of situations and people.

Have Fun

Guiding is about having fun and creating an enjoyable experience for your visitors. They have joined your walk to have a good time, so they are ready for an enjoyable experience.

Love of People

If you are warm, friendly, and have a genuine love of people, this will help your visitors feel that you really care about them. It is always a good idea to ask, before you start each walking tour, if anyone has any special needs, so you can ensure you consider and include all your guests.

Anticipate Needs

The handling of complaints is always a challenge, so having an ability to anticipate needs and concerns; and then manage them, is also an important trait of a guide.

Communication

You are enthusiastic about your topic, so show this in your verbal and non-verbal communication and interpersonal skills. You have the capacity to make the experience so much nicer for both you and your guests. This includes manners and etiquette.

The art of listening is invaluable for a guide to understand and respond to questions.

Adaptable
The ability to change and adapt will reduce your stress and keep the group's enjoyment high. They really do not need to know about all your problems behind the scenes. You can be the duck gliding on the water with those little feet frantically keeping you afloat (if you need to).

A walking tour is like live TV. You need to be able to change your route and adapt your content at any time. A road may be closed, your guests may not be what you expected, or you may have to deal with something unexpected. Of course, you cannot plan for all eventualities, but, if you are versatile, you can sail through most rough seas.

Knowledgeable
A guide has an inquisitive mind, a love of learning and a desire to grow. If you constantly enhance your knowledge (and in a wide range of topics), you will become a better guide, and your tours will become even better. The day you add the last piece to your jigsaw puzzle of learning is the day that you give up guiding.

Love of Learning
Focused and structured learning is important too. Often, tour guides focus on one subject, which can make their tour a bit one-dimensional. It is fine to be a specialist and do walks around a theme but be aware of the gaps in your knowledge. The wider your knowledge base, the more walks you can do. This increases walking tour job offers and repeat business. General walks can be good for tourists and specific themed walks, might be better for locals. So, make yourself a generalist for more opportunities and to make yourself more interesting.

Community-Minded

Understand and know your community. You represent your area and if people ask you questions, you need to have some foundation of knowledge. You may have guests from out of town or even from outside your country. The more you know about life in your community and everyday activities, the more your guests will understand what you are sharing with them.

Cultural Practices and Awareness

Not everyone who comes on your tour will be from your religious background, or from your culture. Never assume anything. Avoid cultural references or humour that would offend. This will also of course, include political views.

Always be objective!

Show patience for those who might not understand your accent or the language you are guiding in, as well as patience for those of different cultures and walks of life.

You may not know everything about other cultures, but at least showing an understanding of cross-cultural differences and a willingness to learn, will also make your job so much easier.

Activity

Here is your opportunity to list the things you are good at, and those skills and qualities that need a bit of work.

But remember: There is a certain type of person who wants to guide, and that is YOU.

You do not have to change who you are, but once you are aware of something that could improve, you start to enhance how you come across.

CHAPTER 6: KNOWLEDGE

Without a solid foundation of knowledge, no guide can ever be truly professional.

The main aim of a walking tour is to place the content within a wider context. The buildings, venues, statues, structures, landscape. The idea is to bring out all the ***relevant*** detail.

I must emphasise 'relevant'. Some guides feel that they need to tell their groups everything they know about a topic, which might not be interesting to a lot of people. This might also be quite boring, and drag the walk out, or keep people standing in one place for too long.

Bring out what is relevant and interesting.

You have views and your guests have views about facts and 'facts'. This is how we perceive ourselves and the world in which we live.

Do not just inform. Rather interpret and tell stories. Some of your guests may never have seen what you are going to show them. Others have seen, but not noticed, and maybe not understood. Never presume anything.

Using the phrase, "As you all know…" may alienate those who do not know.

Weave your concepts, language, history, and stories together to appeal to the head and the heart.

Choose your area of expertise and build on it with the art and skill of interpretation.

Tilden's Six Principles of Interpretation

Freeman Tilden is known as the father of interpretation. His six principles come from observing a range of interpretive activities such as guided walks, talks and presentations. These principles can be used effectively in your capacity as a guide when you deliver Heritage Interpretation.

Interpretation of your content should be:

1. *Personal to your audience:* relate as much as possible to your audience
2. *More than just facts:* stories, legends, and experiences
3. *Teachable:* broken down into 'easy to digest' chunks
4. *Stimulating to encourage action*: learning more, going on another tour
5. *Presented as a whole, rather than in parts*: context makes it more enjoyable
6. *Relevant to the group:* ages, interests, and needs

(Tilden, F. 1977. Interpreting Our Heritage. 3rd edition. Chapel Hill: The University of North Carolina Press.)

Make it easy to remember with ORE

ORE (Organised, Relevant and Enjoyable):

Organised

If you spend time organising your walk knowledge into chunks, it will be easier to remember. This also gives a logical sequence to the walk and is easier for your guests to remember and engage with your content. People generally do not remember more than four of five main ideas, so keep your messages short and simple.

Relevant

Your walks should always have meaning for the guests. If you can bring in a personal side for them to relate to, you will be a brilliant guide. This helps connect their lives to the stories and the places they are exploring with you.

Enjoyable
A successful guide makes this a priority. Keep things fun and your guests will leave with a warm feeling about the place you have shared with them.

How do you acquire the necessary knowledge?

Activity

- Find all the books you can about your topic of interest. Your local bookshop will stock them, as well as museums and gift shops.
- There are so many resources online. But be aware of 'fake news', journalist exaggeration and flaws. Cross-check all the information you find online to ensure your information is accurate and up to date.
- Join local groups where these types of lectures will be delivered – history or wildlife groups, for example. Get to as many as you possibly can. Find the most obvious knowledge base needed for your specific tour and to expand the knowledge you already have. You will meet more people in the community which could prove to be valuable relationships when you start leading your walking tours.

CHAPTER 7:
WHAT A GUIDE COULD KNOW & SHARE

What a guide shares on a walking tour is, of course, relevant to the reason and the theme of the walk. Here are the most relevant areas of knowledge to cover on a walking tour.

- *Historic facts* are important, and so are dates. But dates can be overwhelming. Focus on the most important dates and then just ensure that everything else you mentioned is at least in a date sequence. Do not get hung up on the details of dates.
- *Art and architecture* might be relevant if you are in a town.
- *Cultural and traditional history* is always fascinating.
- *Current news* but stay away from controversial topics and keep your views neutral.
- *Memories of events* you experienced yourself and lived through.
- *Geographic information* about natural attractions, such as lakes, waterfalls and mountains will interest those staying in the area for a few days. *Altitude* will help put your area on a map in relation to mountain ranges or distance to the sea. And this will influence the local economy, and other human activity in the area.
- *Climate* and statistics about rainfall and snow will interest locals and visitors, especially if you are able to compare them to other parts of the region, countries, or other parts of the world.
- *Main industries* are topics people love to ask about. They like to know how the region made its money in the past, and how its economy functions today.

Your walking tour is an opportunity to promote other local attractions and activities in town. You can motivate the guests to want to learn more, especially for those staying longer. This might include visits to farms or factories, cycle routes or other outdoor activities. You can find out all this information from your local or regional Tourist Information Centre or your town council.

You might not know about all these activities, but if you at least know the opening and closing times of your Tourist Information Centre, you can send your guests to find out more.

Your walking tour is a promotional tool which will encourage people to spend their money in the hotels, shops, pubs and in the restaurants.

Importantly, many guests will arrive on your tours with preconceived ideas. We live in an Information Age, and we are constantly bombarded with messages from the TV, from the newspapers, from social media. It is worth anticipating what these preconceived ideas are so that you can dispel any 'fake news'.

Your aim is to provide a clear understanding of your town or region and HAVE FUN!

Activity

How can you promote your local community?
- Make a list of all the businesses and organisations you walk past on your walking tours (or plan to walk past)
- Pop in to introduce yourself and let them know you will be taking groups past. Ask them if they would like you to let your group know what they have on offer - maybe it is a pub or a restaurant with local dishes, a bakery, gift shop, museum or gallery.

This is a great way for your local community to know that you are doing local walking tours, and to raise your own profile (which also helps when you are ready to promote your walking tours).

CHAPTER 8: PERSONALITY

Personality makes us all unique and cannot be taught. Thus, some people will make better guides than others.

There is a saying:

"You can be the tastiest peach in the world, and there will still be people who don't like peaches."

We all want to be liked, but there are people who come on your walking tours who will not like you. They may not like your accent, or the way you dress. You might remind them of someone they do not like. All of this is out of your control, but if you do your best to set the tone at the start of your walking tour, you increase the chances of people having a good time. The first five minutes are the most important as this lays the foundations for the rest of the experience.

Show your personality so that your guests feel at ease. This will ensure that your walking tour is enjoyable for you and for them.

"The greatest compliment a guide can receive, is that they are enthusiastic.
And the most damning, is that they are boring."
Katrine Prince

When you guide, you are combining a range of skills.
Two of the most important:
1. The skills of a teacher: being informative and sharing accurate information to ensure you build credibility
2. The energy and enthusiasm of an entertainer: without it being about you

If you have created a positive environment at the very beginning of your tour, and then something goes wrong along the way, you can win the group back quite quickly. It may even prove to be a highlight for them. But if you start off negatively, the group can be very unforgiving. Things will deteriorate as you progress on your tour. This can become a difficult and unpleasant situation for you and for the group.

So, win your guests over, by highlighting your best traits, and with your very first engagement with your visitors, even before you start your walking tour.

Make yourself feel good too. Why not?

Activity

- Ask your friends and family what they think makes you a good walking tour guide. Write these ideas down and put them on the wall (or the fridge) where you can see them. This is the list you can turn to when you feel a bit low, overwhelmed, or despondent.
- Think about what you can tell your group in the first five minutes that will make them respond warmly to you.

We are all different so just BE YOU!
You are going to make a great guide!

CHAPTER 9:
YOUR APPEARANCE FOR CONFIDENCE

Have you ever been to a party and felt under, or over-dressed? It is very awkward, and something I hope never to experience again. Appearance is so important.

Remember, first impressions count.

And it is important to be comfortable too.

So, how do we dress when we are guiding?

Be aware of the different circumstances, groups, and environments where dress codes are important. It is a good idea to ask yourself:
- Am I comfortable? (Shoes, fabric that does not make you sweat, too hot, too cold, hats in windy weather, too tight, too loose?)
- Is my appearance casual, yet professional? (Neat and tidy is important)
- Are my clothes suitable for the location where I am guiding? (In a church you may need to cover shoulders and knees, for example)
- Is it suitable for the guests? (Different themed walks may need different attire, and different types of groups may need a clothing consideration)

When you feel good and look professional, your level of performance increases because you feel more confident. You will naturally guide better, and your guests will have more confidence in you.

Activity

It might be worth going through your wardrobe to see if you have comfortable shoes that look professional. You also want to avoid synthetic fabrics (sweaty armpits are distracting).

If you guide in different seasons, think about an umbrella, raincoat, hat, and if sleeveless shirts / tops are appropriate.

Consider items of clothing that can be used as props (theme them with your walking tour) or to identify you in a crowd.

It feels like a theatre performance, doesn't it?

Well, it sort of is.

CHAPTER 10: NERVOUSNESS

It is normal to be nervous. But the trick is **not** to show that you are nervous. You can learn to control your nerves, so that nobody knows that you are a little unsure.

Actors, professional public speakers; and teachers who stand up in front of a classroom, all get nervous too. And it is a good thing to feel a little bit nervous and have those butterflies in your tummy to increase adrenaline. Adrenaline is good.

But you do not want to be **seen** to be nervous.

So, why would a guide feel nervous?
- There might be an expert in the group. You might recognise them as a specialist by their questions or they have spoken to you before the tour. They may have told you that they are a history professor, an archaeologist, or something that is a field that you will be covering on your walking tour.
- The group could be expert, so, they might be a group of nuns and you will be taking them into a church. They may be artists, and you will be taking them to an art gallery.
- You may feel like you have not had enough time to prepare for your walking tour.
- Maybe you do not feel that you know enough.
- You could be at the very beginning of your career as a walking tour guide.
- There is always the fear of drying up or having a mental block - saying as much as you have in your head and then it is just not enough. Or, for some or other reason, the information is just not there.
- Are you worried about looking silly? Feeling exposed?

These are all very normal feelings. But nervousness will show in our body language.

How do guides show their nerves?

Some people tap their feet. They might shuffle or move around. You might know people who crunch their knuckles or constantly twist their rings. Some guides fidget or put their hands through their hair over and over. A colleague of mine constantly scratched or rub their eyes. I have a friend who readjusts her glasses as a nervous twitch. I know someone who sways and rocks back and forth when she is talking to a group. This can all be very distracting!

When you are nervous, often, your voice quivers, and you find yourself swallowing a lot because your mouth gets very dry.

And it is completely natural to avoid eye contact with the group when you are nervous.

Activity

How do your nerves manifest? Ask those around you too. You may be really surprised.

Being aware of these habits, will help you control them, or at least make them less visible or obvious.

You can take control of your body with some simple tricks and techniques.

CHAPTER 11:
CONTROLLING YOUR NERVES

We all manage our nerves in different ways, and maybe you have found techniques that work well for you. Here are some ideas you might want to try:

1. **Adopt a well-balanced stance.**

Stand with your feet slightly apart and keep your weight evenly distributed on both your hips. It is easy to stand with one hip down and one hip up. But if your spine is straight, you have a more comfortable stance. This will also reduce the tiredness which comes from slouching. And gives you an air of quiet authority. This is of course, extremely helpful for the group to have more confidence in you and what you are going to be doing with them for the next hour (or however long your walking tour is).

2. **Draw your shoulders back with your arms loosely behind you.**

You can even put your hands in your back pockets. I know this is something that most public speaking trainers will say not to do. But in a casual environment like a guided tour, putting your hands in your back pockets will open your chest. It improves your posture by expanding your lungs. And when your lungs expand, you get more oxygen, and this is good for brain function.

3. **Control your hands.**

When your hands are controlled, your movements are controlled. Every movement must be meaningful. So, if you are pointing, do not just wave in a general direction. Make a conscious positive signal if you want your group to look in a certain direction, with a positive gesture. If you want your group to look to your left, you should point to THEIR right (you will be facing them). This is quite tricky to get used to, but it becomes easier as you gain more experience. It even becomes second nature after a while.

4. **Use your hands to describe things.**

Your hands should be free to move. But if you are carrying a bag (or props), make sure they do not limit the use of your hands. You could, however, have a folder with some old images or props to explain a concept. But carry these in a bag on your back or over your shoulder, to keep your hands free to describe and show.

5. **Establish eye contact with the entire group.**

Some guides tend to latch on to people who are showing an interest, or who are asking the most questions. But remember your whole group needs to feel special and know you are speaking to them individually. Be aware of everybody in the group by making sure you look at everyone over the course of the walk.

6. **Take control of your breathing.**

When you control your breathing, you control your nerves and your voice. Nerves make your breathing shallow. When you breath deeper your voice sounds more controlled (and can be used for more emphasis). This will send more oxygen to your brain to help you think clearly.

7. **Have the courage to be silent.**

When you feel you are getting nervous: stop! Take two or three deep breaths. Some of the world's best orators have used pauses to have more of an effect. Once you feel that your body has calmed down, the words will start flowing again.

They really will... I promise.

Activity

- Take each of these points and weave them into your daily engagements with friends, family, and colleagues. Test them out to see if they do reduce your nerves.
- Then ask those around you it if there is a difference to how you show your nerves.

Your goal is to ensure that your nerves do not control you, but that you control how they manifest themselves.

CHAPTER 12:
INVOLVE YOUR GUESTS

You are a 'people person'. You love chatting to people and sharing your knowledge. But some guides treat their walking tours as a sort of a lecture - a one-way conversation. This may be the case for guides who are a little shy. And at the beginning of your guiding career, you may feel that you just do not know enough to involve your guests in the conversation.

You do not have to know everything, and you can tell your guests that too. By getting them involved in your walking tour, you will enhance their experience, and will give you that guiding 'buzz'! Your guests will have a better understanding of what you are trying to share with them. It also keeps their interest high, and they feel special enough to be involved and considered.

Examples:
- Do you have this plant where you are from?
- Are there statues in your hometown?
- How old is your city? Country?
- Do you have something similar in your culture?

Weave the questions into commentary when they are relevant. You will have an idea of where your group is from as you asked these questions at the very beginning of the walk, before you even started moving.

But, it is also your job to know if there are some questions you need to avoid, or subjects that would upset, divide or alienate guests.

Invite your group to ask questions.

Human beings are curious!

Do not be concerned about inviting questions. Most of the time the question will be something you can answer quite easily. If not, you can thank them for asking the question and say you do not know the answer: "That is a very good question and something I have not considered before. I really do not know."

You may be able to answer the question using your knowledge and the powers of deduction. Or you could also refer them to a website, an information centre or a book where they could find the answer.

You could even throw the question out to the group to ask if anyone else knows the answer. This takes a lot of confidence too, but if you feel you can 'wow' your group in other ways, I think this is a lovely way to get your group chatting. But, if you think you have a 'know it all' or a show-off in your group, it may be better to avoid asking the group for their answer to a question. It will only give this person the space to interfere in your walk.

Getting your guests involved in the walking tour, will bond the group, and makes for a much more fun and positive environment for everyone.

Overall, be aware of your group and adapt your walk according to your skills, confidence, and your group's needs and knowledge. Every group will be different, so not all tactics will work with every group.

Be yourself and be confident in what you know and can share.

You have prepared, researched, and practised so be confident that you know more than your group. They may be a specialist in their field, but you are a specialist in yours – being a guide.

Activity

When you are preparing your walking tour, think of ways to encourage mini discussions in a couple of places along your route. You do not want a debate, but rather simple questions to make the walk a conversation, rather than a lecture. Ensure that these discussions do not impact on the length of the walking tour either or take you off topic.

If chats are impacting on your walking tour, invite guests to stay afterwards and continue the conversation.

As you gain more experience and confidence, this kind of conversation will come naturally, and you will not need to consciously think about them.

CHAPTER 13: HUMOUR

We all love a good laugh. I bet you have told a joke in a social situation, and then wished you had not told it. Your joke may have fallen flat, or it offended, and you did not expect it to. It is vital that you consider humour in your guiding.

Humour is quite tricky. It is fine, and encouraged, to make the odd comment or draw a parallel to something fun.

Jokes should be used with caution.

Remember that different nationalities laugh at different things. Some people can be quite critical about what is funny and what is not funny. And if you forget the punchline, or you realise halfway through that the joke is not relevant, it could be embarrassing for you and / or your guests.

If you do find a joke that works and that you can use with sensitivity, go ahead.

But never make a joke at the expense of somebody else and be careful not to offend anybody in your joke. Generally, it is probably best to consider other ways to make your group smile or even laugh.

Please do not panic if you do not think you are funny. You do not need to be funny to be a guide. All you need is to be friendly, open, informative and YOURSELF!

Barry Hilton, a well-known South African comedian, shares his three types of jokes:

1. Pun – a play on words
Example: *Being a walking tour guide in Kensington Gardens is a 'walk in the park'*

2. Exaggeration – take to extremes
Example: *Every orange in the country was inspected for the king's marmalade.*
3. False Logic – misdirection
Example: *William the Conqueror rounded up his troops by sending a WhatsApp message to the group called '1066 Invasion'.*

You will be surprised to know that you can create your own jokes. You can also use jokes that you have heard from others to enhance your walking tour but be aware of how they (and you) come across. The joke might not have the same effect when you deliver it.

There is a saying in the guiding community:

"A guide who is too intent on information risks becoming boring. And the guide who is too intent on entertaining, risks becoming a Prima Donna."
Anonymous

Activity

When you are planning your walking tour, add in a couple of your own, or others' jokes, that would fit in at different points on your walk. Try and weave your jokes in, seamlessly alongside other ways to win your guests over by making them smile.

Humour is a fine balance, which will come with experience too.

Section 3: Presenting

CHAPTER 14: BODY LANGUAGE

With so much of our message coming from our body language, it is so important to be aware of how we stand, walk, and communicate.

It is not very friendly to:
- *Cross your arms across your chest:* this can be seen as defensive.
- *Hold your hands on your hips:* this denotes a certain aggression.
- *Have your hands in your front pockets:* this give people the impression you are not actually taking things seriously.
- *Lean* against a wall, a pole, statue, or a car: it looks unprofessional
- *Fix your gaze* on just one person: this tends to be embarrassing for them.

It is so much friendlier to:
- *Stand tall* with confidence (even if you do not feel it).
- *Allow your arms to swing* naturally when you move or stand still.
- **Make EYE contact with everyone in the group**, even if just briefly. This will put everyone at ease. They will all feel like you are speaking directly to them. But take note of the shy person, the person on their own, or struggling to keep up. Eye contact helps to bond with everyone in friendly way.

Make eye contact as often as you can and with the whole group (not just those who are demanding your attention).

Activity

Ask your friends and family if there is something you do that your group will notice: a nervous twitch or if you sway, for example.

Be aware of it. It is not bad or wrong, as long as it does not distract you from delivering a great walking tour.

Importantly, be aware of cultural differences. In some cultures, it is rude to look directly into the eyes, or it may be an insult to touch.

Be sensitive to how you are coming across.

A smile on your face is a smile in your voice.

CHAPTER 15: USING YOUR HANDS

Some of us need our hands to fully express ourselves when we talk. But when you are leading a walking tour, try to control your hands. Do what it takes to keep your hands from being distracting.

Every movement should be meaningful.

If you are pointing, do not wave in a general direction. Consider a conscious, positive signal for your guests to look in a specific direction.

When your hands are controlled, your movements are controlled.

Gesture positively.

Remember: you will not be carrying notes, but you may want to show your group images or use props to enhance the experience. It is best to have a bag that does not limit the use of your hands.

When you use your hands to point, show and tell, it is good for those who are hard of hearing, or those who do not speak the language you are guiding in. They will get a clearer picture of what you are talking about.

Activity

In your everyday life, start using phrases like 'YOUR right' and then gesturing according to the person facing you.

It may seem a bit odd to start with, but with practice, it will become second nature.

CHAPTER 16:
KNOW YOUR VOICE

Your voice is an incredible tool, and an invaluable instrument for your guiding.

You can train your voice to be even more effective, but it also needs to be looked after and nurtured. A strong, solid, clear, and well-projected voice will enhance your walking tour. It will be easier for your guests to follow your commentary which means they will of course, enjoy it more.

When communicating with a group, speak loudly (without shouting), clearly (be aware of your accent) and controlled to convey your passion and excitement.

A boring voice takes away so much from your colourful stories.

Clarity

To articulate clearly, your consonants need to be crisp and clean, and your vowels need to sound as pure as possible. When you are nervous, you may speak through clenched teeth, and you will thus lose clarity of speech. You are less likely to speak through clenched teeth when you feel prepared. But this will change as you get more experience.

Variety

You are a storyteller and variety in your voice can create drama to bring your stories alive. You can achieve variety in your voice by changing your pitch, volume, and the speed of your speech, which you will need to practise. But overall, focus on speaking slowly and clearly. Speeding up may help awaken a sleepy audience, for example, if they have got off a coach, after a long journey.

Speed can also create an element of surprise.
Emphasis can be achieved by dropping your voice to speak slower or quietly.

Silence

Silence raises expectations and creates suspense and drama. Do not be afraid to use silence. It can also be used very effectively if you have people talking at the back of the group. When they hear that you are not talking, they tend to stop too. They could be distracting the others and taking away from the overall enjoyment of your walking tour.

Breathing correctly

Your diaphragm is where you should breathe from.
You do not want to use your vocal cords to increase volume. This will result in shouting and a strained voice. So, to increase the volume, maintain deep breathing and then push the volume out on the ***exhale breath***.

Place your hands on your ribcage. Breathe in deeply through your nose and out through your mouth. If you feel your ribs moving in and out with every breath inhaled and exhaled, then you are breathing most effectively. Concentrate on breathing with depth, slowly and intentionally.

Shallow, sporadic breathing heightens your nervousness. Nerves can play a big role in how you breathe, and your breathing can play a big role in how nervous you are. But remember, this is just temporary. You have the capacity to change this as soon as you become aware of it.

If you notice that your breathing is shallow while you are in front of a group, pause, relax your shoulders to instantly open your ribcage, and take control of your breathing. Just a few deep breaths will help you to use your voice better. As soon as you start breathing slowly and deeply it makes it easier to talk, and your brain fog will clear away.

You can do this before you start with any commentary or even when you are walking from one stop to the next.

If you use your voice badly, incorrectly, or put strain on your vocal cords, for a considerable length of time, you can cause serious and long-term damage. And eventually, the vocal cords will struggle to function, and you will lose your voice. The only suggestion at this point is to rest. You may also need medical intervention for removal of nodules.

To prevent this from happening, make sure you are aware of your voice, how you use it and how it feels. You should also take regular breaks to rest your voice by not speaking at all.

A guide needs a voice! It is thus advisable to know and understand breathing techniques so you can protect your voice.

Being Heard

It is vital that you are heard! This might sound obvious, but often guides do not consider *how* they are being heard.

Volume should not come from your throat. It needs to come from the exhalation of your breath.

Pitch your commentary to reach those furthest away from you. Do this with your voice, eye contact and your brain. If you focus on the people right in front of you or the people standing just within reaching distance, those on the extremities of the group will struggle to hear you. They may lose interest and drop off your walking tour.

If you try to pitch too far and too loud, your voice could become a shriek, which is not comfortable for people to listen to.

Focus on:
- Speaking loudly (without shouting)
- Changing the pace of your sentences
- Speaking quietly but so that people a few metres away can still hear you

Activity

- Practise breathing deeply regularly, so that it becomes easier and natural for you.
- Prepare your commentary in front of a mirror. Be conscious of mouthing your vowels, so that you can start working those muscles (the same muscles you would use if you were singing). It might even ache at first but, like any muscle, your mouth will become quite fit.
- Normally no group will extend beyond 20 feet from where you are standing. Get a friend to stand 20 feet away from you and practise your commentary, without shouting, to make sure they can hear you.

CHAPTER 17:
HOW TO BE HEARD

You want to give your group the best opportunity to hear what you have to say **and** see what you are talking about.

When your group struggles to hear you, they lose interest, and it is very difficult to 'get them back'.

Here are a few pointers:

Move in Close
Get the group to move in close to you so that they can all hear you (and to protect your voice), before you start talking. Ask if they can all hear you clearly. If you can see them all, they can see you. Make sure you are in the line of everyone. This may seem like a lot to think about, but it does come naturally with experience.

The larger your group, the slower you need to talk to ensure everyone can hear you.

Face Your Group
You should try as much as possible to ***face your group***. Your ***left*** becomes their ***right***, so keep this in mind when you are pointing things out. If you have guests who are hard of hearing, they will be grateful to be able to lip-read. Those who do not speak the language you are guiding in, as their first language, will also find it easier to look at you so they do not miss anything.

Use your Breath
When you need to increase your volume, use your breath, (force the volume out as you exhale), rather than exerting your vocal cords, which can become shouting. This is unpleasant for your group and not good for your voice.

In Front of You
It is not always possible, but your group should be *in front of you*. If the group starts to 'creep' behind you, stand with your back up against a wall or a smaller object such as a tree or a pole.

Sound Board / Reflector
If you are in a noisy street, you can make it easier for your group to hear you if you ***create a sound board***. Depending on what the group should be looking at, they can be shepherded against a wall. Then you face the group and the wall. Your voice will bounce off the wall and into the group.

Always have a Plan B to position the group if the one you wanted to use is not available when you arrive there with your group.

Is your group comfortable?
If it is a hot day, move them into the shade, for example. If there is a disturbance, move them away from the commotion. Consider how they feel at every point of the tour.

Activity
Before you take a group out on a walking tour, spend time on the route at that time of the day. You will get an idea of the noisy spots and the congested places which could make it difficult to stop a group.

Plan where you want your group to stand, so that they can see what you are showing and telling them.

Please look after your voice. A strained voice can lead to all sorts of problems and remember, without a voice, you cannot guide.

CHAPTER 18: BARRIERS TO COMMUNICATION

You can be fully prepared and confident before your walking tour, but there may still be situations that could prove to be a barrier to your communication. Some of these you can prevent before your walking tour. But there are times when you just need to be aware of the challenges, so you can adapt as you go along.

Physical Objects
This could be road works barriers, parked cars obstructing your route or an incident where the road has been cordoned off.

Solutions: If you can do a practice walk before you go out with your group, you can work your way around some of these challenges. But, if you arrive at a spot and there is a car parked where you need to walk your group, or show them something, which you no longer have access to, this is more challenging.

If you have told them about this aspect of the tour, and they are unable to see it, explain what it is, tell them what they need to know (limit the information if they cannot see what you are talking about) and let them know how they can come back another time.

Many times, they will have no idea what you were going to show them, and you can just skip it completely. They will never know. And if someone asks about it, you can direct them there after the tour.

Background Noises
If you plan your walk ahead of time, you may not be aware of an increase in traffic at a certain time of the day. Construction can also be very noisy and a passing ambulance or a police siren.

Solutions: If it is possible to walk past the noise, it is best to stop the group at another spot where they can hear you better.

They may not be in the perfect spot to see what you are talking about, but at least they can hear what you have to say. If it is a temporary noise, stop talking and wait for it to pass.

Disruptions / Distractions
This could be a noisy child on the tour, or a guest who is constantly disrupting your flow.

Solutions: This is really challenging, and you need to evaluate your own circumstances and your own character. If you have a guest who keeps asking questions, you could say something like this:

"I don't want to run out of time as I have so much more to share with you on this tour, so if you do have a question, please wait until we start moving to the next stop, and I will happily answer it en route"

It is worth a try, but test what works for you.

Distance between the Guide and the Group
It is very common for your guests to stand quite far away from you. It could be that they do not want to be at the front of the group. They may be tall and feel they would block the view for everyone else. They may be concerned the guide will ask them something, or maybe they think it is polite.

Solutions: Always ask the group to move in closer before you start talking. You can make a joke about it ("most tour guides don't bite"). Or you could say something about not having to shout and if they come closer, they can all hear. If you mention it at the first few stops, your group will be trained quite quickly.

And be clear about exactly where you want them to stand when you stop.

Information
Inaccurate, distorted, subjective (political, ethical,

religious) information could make for an uncomfortable experience for you and your guests. Content that does not make sense, or comes from a secondary source, could also be confusing.

Solutions: Be prepared and do your research (cross-check and fact check your information too). When you start your guiding career, you will have less knowledge than you would like. But, if you know what you want to say, when you want to say it, and know more than your guests, then you will be fine.

Less is more!

You will not know how to answer all the questions, but time and experience will be your friend. Be honest about what you know, and your guests will love their walk with you. Do not assume everyone shares your values, beliefs, goals, and views either. Be as neutral as you can and offer other sources of information if you get questions that take you off in a direction you do not feel comfortable about.

Stress
Negative emotions and how you manifest stress or nerves, can influence how you deliver your walking tours.

Solutions: The best advice is to be as prepared as you can. As you gain more experience, you will get more comfortable, and your stress will decrease. Remember to enjoy it too! Your guests want to have fun and they are more likely to have fun if you are also having a good time!

Language Barriers
It is your responsibility to accommodate differences which can be tricky. But it may not always be realistic. Some words have multiple meanings, and you may have an accent that your guests are not familiar with.

Solutions: Avoid generalisation and stereotyping. Be conscious of putting words into context to make them easier to understand. Be aware of different interpretations. Be sure to ask those who may not be fluent in your language if they understand throughout your walk. Speak slowly and offer explanation if you sense you are not being understood.

Malfunctioning Equipment (microphones)
If you do have access to microphones and headsets for your guests, it is a good idea to carry batteries. But if your microphone breaks and you cannot repair it, you need to make it work without the technology. Bring the group in closer and continue as normal.

It feels like a million things to think about. Please do not feel overwhelmed. The most important elements of a walking tour is that you are prepared and that you and your guests have fun!

Activity
Make time to do a 'dry run' of your walking tour before you meet your group, so that you can avoid as many of the barriers to effective communication as you possibly can.

With bigger physical barriers, you may have to re-think your route, even if just temporarily, which could mean additional research. You want to be clear about where you are going and have all the information covered for your alternate route.

CHAPTER 19: EFFECTIVE COMMUNICATION

When you consider yourself as a host, your guests will always feel welcome.

Effective communication will give you, the guide, an opportunity to share valuable information about your town / region / area and you will be inspired to learn and experience even more.

It is a great idea to consider the information you share, in a local context, and weave it into a really good story.

Effective communication is about being at ease with:

- All types of people
- Range of ages
- Various language groups
- People with a range of interests
- Different levels of knowledge

Other communication skills include:

- *Non-verbal messages and symbols*

These can help in all communication scenarios.

- *Being an active listener*

You will need to be able to 'read' what the group is interested in. Be open to ideas, suggestions, discussions, and other points of view. Give your group space to talk. Do not interrupt them but use your skill to manage the conversation instead.

- *Interpreting feedback*

Understand how to interpret feedback, positively. Learn to 'read' responses from your group. This also comes with experience. 'Reading' a response will help you identify if your group needs to move on to the next stop, or if the group wants more detail. The best way to assess this, if you are unsure, is to ask the group. Their response should be able to direct you in the right direction.

Effective communication will also ensure you keep your group safe. When you build a trusting relationship, they will know that you have their safety as a priority too.

Keep your communication simple and clear. Using jargon can also alienate your group and your accent, slang and local expressions may not be easy for your group to follow. You could explain local 'isms' as part of your commentary, which is always a topic of interest.

> **"Remember that communication is as much a matter of human relations, as it is about transmitting facts"**
> **Anonymous**

Activity

Be honest with yourself in this task:

- Which of the points covered in this chapter are not your strong traits? (Of course, you cannot be brilliant at everything, but there may be a few points you can work on, which will help you communicate a bit better).
- Write them down and see if you can work on those when you communicate with friends and family. This kind of practice will have a positive impact on your guiding.

CHAPTER 20: COMMUNICATING WITH YOUR GUESTS

When a visitor speaks, give them your undivided attention. Stop what you are doing, turn and face them; make eye-contact and respond verbally. Acknowledge their importance.

Thank them for asking the question. Confirm interpretation of what has been asked to ensure you understand. Then you can answer their question appropriately. But, of course, if you do not know the answer, admit that you do not know the answer.

If you are not clear about what they are asking – ask again.

And remember you can repeat things to ensure that they are clear, and that they understand exactly what it is that you are trying to explain.

In all communications, test for feedback. If your guests give you the appropriate feedback, you know that they have understood.

Overview

- Be clear and concise.
- Use the correct language with simple sentences and unambiguous words.
- Avoid unnecessary jargon or local slang unless of course you are weaving it into a story. A word or expression that is a local term can be a very interesting part of your commentary.
- Be comprehensive, but precise. Remember: less is more.
- Say exactly what you mean.
- Ensure there is a logical sequence to your commentaries.
- Be aware of your pronunciation.
- Focus on projecting your voice so that the whole group

can receive your message.
- Constantly ask if people can hear you before you continue with your commentary.
- Be confident.
- Know your product by continuing your research and making sure that your information is correct, and from reliable sources. Cross-check your information for accuracy.
- Be proud of your town or region. You are the link between the visitors and the area. You represent your community.
- Share local news such as house prices - people love house prices.
- Be respectful helpful and polite. Remember, everyone in the group deserves the same attention, even if they are challenging, have expressed a different view or a different opinion.
- Be a leader, without being bossy. Rather show leadership.
- Pay attention to nonverbal cues such as body language, posture, gestures, and facial expressions. They all send a message.
- Focus on making your content appropriate by making sure that your message fits the audience and the purpose of your tour. Remember that you are pitching to the interests and expectations of your group.
- Be positive. Share negatives in a positive light.

It is easy to say:
"How annoying that the museum is closed today."

You could rather say:
"As the museum is closed today, I will have time to show you one of my favourite hidden treasures in town."

It is easy to say:
"I am so sorry we only have an hour together. That is just not enough time for you to see very much."

You could rather say:
"I am thrilled I get to spend an hour with you to show some of the best highlights of our special town!"

Activity

Think about how you can incorporate each of the points mentioned, into your walking tour. Some of them you could consciously build into your commentary. Others may need to be 'woven' into the full experience.

CHAPTER 21: ASSESS YOUR DELIVERY

How do we know that we have communicated effectively?

1. **Interpersonal relationships**

You will know when your communication has improved. You will see positive communication between the individuals in the group, the support staff, and suppliers such as at the Tourist Information Centre, venues, shops, and restaurants that you take the group into or that you recommend.

2. **If the group asks questions**

When the group is engaged with your content (asking questions and participated in discussions), you know that they feel fulfilled and happy. You want your group to leave your walking tour with more knowledge. You will not always know how exactly how they feel, but you should be able to read their feelings in their manner, and how they respond to you in the long-term (on social media and feedback, for example).

3. **If your walking tours are full and you get bookings**

Word-of-Mouth and referrals are still the most powerful form of marketing.

4. **Feedback**

Ivor Armstrong Richards used the term 'feedforward'. The information you receive after your walking tours should always be seen as positive ways to improve. If you receive positive and enthusiastic feedback/ feedforward, analyse it carefully.

5. **You Receive Tips**

You might be lucky enough, at the end of your walking tour, to receive a financial tip. But this is not a good measure of your tour because some cultures tip and some cultures do not consider this a reasonable way to show their appreciation. Some will even tip if it was a bad experience (because it is just what they do), and some will tip even if they think it was okay. There are people who will be reluctant to tip because 'We already paid for the walk' or they may feel that a tip is an insult.

If you do receive a tip, think about it as a welcome bonus and not a measure of your success or failure.

Consider the following:
- If tipping is part of *your* culture, it might be worth building that into your commentary, like when you are talking about a local restaurant.
- If tipping is not part of your culture, but might be for your guests, you can consider how you will make it easier for them to tip you.

6. Self-Assessment

Analysis of your own perceptions will help you become a better guide.

Ask yourself:
- Did I pitch my message at the right level?
- Was it too fact heavy?
- Was the pace right for the group?
- Did the group look like they enjoyed the walk?
- Did the guests look bored at any point?
- Did people learn something new?
- Was the information relevant to the theme of the walking tour?
- Why would the group want to know what I have shared with them?
- ***Would I enjoy my own walking tour?***

Ask your group if the answers are not obvious:
"What did you enjoy the most?"

Overview

Are topics on your walking tour an opportunity for you to share something that might reflect your own views?

Focus on the bigger picture. Keep your ideas fresh by continuing to question your own views.

Make sure you include the 'other side' of the discussion so that you have not made it obvious what your views are. Seek to embrace other angles and incorporate your scope of perception.

If your assessment is not great

Do not be concerned if something goes wrong. You can learn from your mistakes and improve with every walking tour. Your group wants to have fun, so maintain a sense of humour and perspective.

They are already enjoying themselves before they start – they are on holiday or spending leisure time doing something interesting. A guide is only as successful as each separate tour. So, if you've had a bad tour before this one, it does not mean that this tour is going to be a disaster. Take time to reflect on whether your group really did enjoy the tour - if you were aware that they enjoyed it but also that you enjoyed it.

Activity

Spend some time thinking about how you were influenced and where your views come from. This has a huge impact on how you come across when you are guiding. You do not want to alienate your guests so, find ways to embrace other views to widen your perceptions and inform them too. There is so much noise and falsehoods on social media. Your job is not to influence your guests to change their views, but to offer an overview and different perspectives.

Section 4: Your Group

CHAPTER 22: VISITOR EXPECTATIONS

In Chapter 2: What is a Walking Tour? we covered some of the reasons why people go on a walking tour. It might be obvious why they are on your walking tour. But, in Chapter 3: the Story of Shula, one of the first things Shula did, was ask her guests some questions. She thus understood what her guests were expecting from her walking tour.

When you are clear about your guests and their expectations, you feel confident with your knowledge, Your next step is to adapt the subject matter to the audience on the day.

Factors to Consider
- Nationality
- Country of origin
- Age
- Gender
- Socio-economics
- Education
- Special interests

Questions you can ask your group
You want to assess how much they already know so you know how to pitch your content. It is amazing how much information you can draw from and about your guests by asking some simple, conversational questions:
- *How long is your visit in the town?*
- *Have you been here before?*
- *Where else have you been?*
- *Where are you going after the walking tour?*

If the walking tour is a pre-booked tour, or if people have booked directly with you (they may even be accompanied by a tour manager / director), you can get a lot of visitor information before the walking tour starts.

The best source of this information about the visitors, is from them directly. So, allow time at the beginning of your walking tour (while you are waiting for more people to join, or for people to return from using the facilities) to chat and find out as much as you can. Gauging the group by asking some chatty questions will also break the ice.

Fulfil the Promises

Brochures, itineraries, flyers, posters, websites, and social media posts all make promises about your walking tour. It is important to deliver what has been promised, even if you think you may want to adapt the walking tour according to the group you have in front of you. You have an obligation to deliver what your guests have been sold.

If a specific route has been advertised, it should be followed, unless completely impossible (which will cover you legally). If a time has been set for the length of the tour, keep to that time. This can be difficult when people ask questions along the way, (which of course you will love), but it is important to be firm with your time. Let your group know that they can continue the discussion at the end of the tour. That way those who need to leave on time, can leave, and those who would like to stay and chat, have that option too.

There may be some practical things your guests could ask. With experience, you could weave this information into your walking tour:

- *Where can they buy stamps?*
- *Where are the public facilities?*
- *What is the local dish?*
- *Where can they buy a typical souvenir of the town?*
- *Where can they have lunch?*

- *Is there public transport?*

Try as much as you can to over-deliver on content.

Activity

Ask yourself these questions:
- Why do you go on a walking tour when you are exploring a new area?
- What do you love the most about a walking tour?
- What bad experiences have you had on a walking tour?
- Write down a list of reasons why you would want to do a walking tour in your town, region, or area.

Ask friends and family and even previous visitors to your town, village, or area, why they went on a walking tour in your area. If they have not done a walking tour in the area, ask them why not, and what they would want from a walking tour for them to sign up for one.

Being conscious of why THEY are there, helps you to be more aware of why YOU are there. This will have an impact on the expectations your guests have, as well as the expectations you place on yourself.

CHAPTER 23:
GROUP MANAGEMENT

If your group cannot hear or see you, they will lose interest. Every time you stop to speak to your group, make sure you position yourself, and the group, for the best opportunity for you to be seen and heard.

Most importantly, do not stand in-front of what you are talking about. You will be blocking the view for your group. Position yourself to the side so that the view becomes the focus, and not you. This is especially important if you are in a museum, an art gallery, or any other large room.

Choose your place with the following considerations:

1. Your group needs to be out of the way of the public or the activities in the room. You do not want to make a nuisance of yourself, or you may not be allowed back next time.
2. Everyone in the group can see and hear you.
3. Everyone can get the best view of what you are talking about.
4. You are in the right place to point out the features of the room or the item you are talking about.
5. If you have a large group, and what you are describing is small, you should start with sharing your information making sure everyone can see and hear YOU. Then ask those in front to have a look at the item and make way for those at the back to file past to see what you have described. Remind the group that you will move away and let them know where you will meet them when they have all seen what you wanted them to see.

Unable to Stop at your Desired Spot

Sometimes you will not be able to stop at something you want to show the group. It may be an important element and relevant to your walking tour. It could be because the object is small, difficult to see, or it is awkwardly positioned. There may be a big crowd or access has been blocked.

The best thing is to mention it at the previous stop. Explain exactly where they will see the object. For example:

"Between the two walls on the left-hand side, under the tree."

Let them know where you will meet them afterwards. They can file past the object or the site and meet you on the other side.

Do not forget to build this time into your walking tour so that you do not overrun.

While Walking

If you give information while you are walking from stop to stop, only those close to you will hear you. If there is something important (and maybe unexpected) you would like to point out, stop the group, wait for those at the back to catch up and only then share the information.

If you need to cross a road, gather your group at a safe place to cross. Cross the road as a group. If you get across and half the group does not, they will take a chance and try to cross on their own for fear of losing you.

If you know the whole group will not get across together, let them know you will wait for them on the other side. They will feel a lot more comfortable about waiting at the traffic light if they know you will not continue the walk without them.

Activity

When preparing your walking tour, work out where you would like your group to stand at every stop. It might not be obvious at first. Also, identify places where the group might not hear you. There might be a lot of traffic, construction, an event or you may be in a busy thoroughfare.

Spend some preparation time thinking about managing the group so they can always see and hear you.

CHAPTER 24: ANSWERING QUESTIONS

It takes confidence to invite your guests to ask questions or contribute to your walking tour. If you have guests with a lot more knowledge than you have, do not feel threatened. It is your tour, and you will always find a way to 'wow' and charm them.

Questions can be annoying. If you can identify why the person asked the question, you can work around it to limit or reduce the impact they have on the rest of your group. And most importantly, you do not want that one annoying person to ruin the experience for everyone else.

Why are questions annoying?
- They might interrupt the flow of your commentary.
- It could be an irrelevant question.
- The question may pre-empt something you are about to say.
- The person asking is showing off or trying to catch you out.
- Maybe they are deliberately trying to be provocative or rude.
- Maybe you just do not know how to answer the question and you may feel flustered.

"What if they ask me something I don't know?"

Of course, that is going to happen. Probably more so in the early days of your guiding. But it is important to encourage them to ask questions and engage with your information. They are there to learn from you and to have fun, so include them as much as you can.

When a guest does speak to you, **be an active listener!**

- Show that you are happy about being asked a question
- Stop what you are doing and give your full and undivided attention
- Turn to face the person asking the question.
- Make eye contact.
- Let the speaker finish asking their question. It is easy to think we know the question, we answer it, and discover it was not the question after all.
- Repeat the question being asked, so that the whole group can hear and benefit from the answer: "This lady here has asked….". If you make the question and answer only between you and the person asking, you will lose the rest of the group.
- Acknowledge their input and thank them for asking the question. You do not want them to feel stupid for asking something.
- Do not be afraid to ask them to repeat the question if you are not clear. This also gives them an opportunity to reword their question.
- You can also ask for clarification to give you additional information which confirms your understanding of the question, and you can thus answer succinctly.

There is NO stupid question! You want them to feel confident about asking you something they do not know.
Deal gently and professionally with ignorance

Techniques for Answering a Question

You are unique and your relationship with your guests will be different to other tour guides. But here are a few tips you can use to enhance your experience as well as the experience of your guests.

1. Refocus the question

There might be parts of the question you can answer, so focus on what you do know.

2. Build a bridge

You can use the question to direct the answer to something you were going to talk about anyway. You are using the question as a 'bridge' to your own content.

3. Use a Funnel

Acknowledge the wider subject of the question but use the question to narrow your words. This will direct your audience's attention to something you would prefer to spotlight.

Give your answer

Keep your answer short and simple. Focus on being concise! Sometimes being straightforward is best.

Make sure you give an answer!

Remember that a long response could lead to another commentary, and you do not have the time to lose the focus of the walking tour you have prepared.

The 5P's to Answering Questions:

- **Positive**: always reply with a positive answer and be positive about the question and your guest.
- **Poised**: sometimes you might feel a bit 'thrown off' by the question but keep your cool.
- **Polite**: even if the guest is pushing you to have a negative opinion or to get you into a controversial topic, remain polite.
- **Professional:** you are a representative of your area, region, town, city, and your company. You are also part of a large community of tour guides, so by keeping things professional, means you are keeping the high standards that are expected around the world.

- **Prepared**: It is a really good idea to prepare 10 of the *most likely questions* that you are going to be asked, should they arise.

If you do not know the answer

Always admit that you do not know something. If you try to make something up or bumble through an answer, it will reflect badly on you.

Instead, offer them some other information that relates to their question. And remind them that their question is a very good and valid question, which may be something you have not thought about and that you will investigate.

Research the answers to all questions you could not answer. If one guest has asked the question, no doubt others will too. This is a great way to build your knowledge and to ensure that when someone asks it next time, you know the answer.

It takes courage to admit you do not know, and it makes you look more professional and human too.

Activity

- Use your friends and family to identify possible questions. Ask them what they would like to know. Share your information with them and ask if it is clear and easy to understand.
- Research and prepare likely questions so you are fully prepared for them next time.

The more you research, the better your guiding will be. Research will become one of your favourite parts of guiding.

CHAPTER 25: DIFFICULT QUESTIONS

There will always be one difficult customer. Your task is to manage them to prevent their behaviour from having an impact on you and your group.

You may need to take your difficult customer aside and ask for them to work with you to make the tour a pleasant experience for everyone. It is always best to solve the problem without spoiling the whole group's experience.

These are a few techniques you may want to try:
- To avoid questions that interrupt or are irrelevant, fix a time for questions in advance. Plan these times into your tour. It could be at a certain point in the walk, or it could be at the end of every stop. You may want to limit questions to the very end of the walk, especially if you are on a tight schedule.
- Repeating of the question is so important because in this instance, the show-off or the silly question, will be shown up. Often others in the group will provide the answer to a silly question, which solves the problems for you.
- Provocative or offensive questions should be politely sidestepped.
- If you do not know the answer, admit it and thank them for asking such a great question. Offer to find out or direct them to where they can find the answer, or you could lose credibility, especially if someone in the group knows the answer.
- Do not avoid or ignore a difficult question.
- If you do give your opinion in an answer, make sure that you say that it is your opinion and not a fact.

You will aggravate the situation by being rude or angry, or panicking, lying, snapping, or putting the person down in front of the others.

No guide can ever know everything! There will be times when you will not know the answer, but hopefully these will become less and less. But, it will never end, because there is always something new to learn.

The best mantra for difficult situations is:

> *"Be cool. Be calm and arm with charm."*
> *Katrine Prince*

Activity

Talk to some experienced tour guides about how they manage different situations. Learn from them.

Section 5: Your Walking Tour

CHAPTER 26: YOUR PRIMARY SUBJECT

As with any content you create or pull together, you need to decide on the primary subject of your walking tour:

- *What do you want your guests to learn?*
- *What do you want them to see?*
- *What do you want them to experience?*

You might want to build a specialist walk, for example, of the pubs in your town. So, your focus will be on putting the information of the pubs into context such as the history of the town.

Start your research by creating a firm foundation of your primary topic, the central idea, or the main subject (such as pub history). This will create a framework, like a jigsaw puzzle. You always start with the border of the puzzle. So, if you have decided to do a walking tour that is mostly historic, then focus on building your historic knowledge first and only then think about adding secondary topics.

It might be overwhelming at first. But keep your focus on the main topic of your walk and start learning. As you start to 'build the jigsaw puzzle' your knowledge will, over time, fill in the gaps. Start simple and let your tour evolve.

Remember, you know a lot more than your guests, even if you are just starting out. You have done lots of reading, seen films, you have researched your topic, it is something you have an interest in, or you live there. Even if you have a history professor on your tour, you still know more about the place where you are guiding.

Walking Tour Guiding

Your guests are always starting from a much lower knowledge base than you are, so do not throw everything at them, and do not panic about what you need to know.

Putting the walk together is always so much fun. You get to physically explore, speak to people who have relevant information, and you get to read and research around the subject that you love.

Activity

- Take a walk around your town, community or area and identify the most obvious theme or primary subject for your walking tour.
- Ask others who live locally what they think would make a good, themed walking tour.
- Choose a primary subject for your first walking tour that is not too obscure. You want information that is easily accessible and a topic that is easy to research.

CHAPTER 27:
ADD TO YOUR JIGSAW

Knowledge forms the foundation of guiding.
It is important that you constantly enhance your knowledge, even if you think you know a lot about a certain subject. There is always something more to learn and you can never know everything!

If your knowledge is a jigsaw puzzle, keep adding pieces to fill the gaps.

> "The day the last piece is placed in the jigsaw is the day to give up being a guide"
> Katrine Prince

According to Katrine Prince, the **first requirement** of a guide is to have an inquisitive mind and the **second requirement** is the love of knowledge across a wide range of subjects.

Your tours might be focused on attracting people from 'out of town', but if you have a wide knowledge base, you will find locals coming to join you too.

Contemporary and local information is interesting, but it is equally important to remain objective. You do not want to upset people with your viewpoint, and you do not want to give people information that will sway them in a certain direction.

Take every opportunity you can, to learn. When you feel confident with a specific topic, offer yourself as a speaker to your local history group, the library or to groups where your topic is of interest. This not only gives you practise, but it raises your profile as the local tour guide. In the virtual world that the 2020 Covid-19 Pandemic has thrown upon us, we can now reach more people globally, which is very exciting.

And of course, your culture is special too. It might be worth researching why you do certain things. We often behave in a specific way and have no idea why.

For example:
- Why do we drive on the left or the right side of the road?
- What is a polite greeting?

Visitors also loving hearing about how people live:
- What is the cost of a house?
- How much is a pint of beer?
- Or a McDonalds burger?
- How big is the church congregation?
- How does the school system work?
- What is the average income?

There is no point putting content into your walk for the sake of it. Give everything context and make it all relevant to what they can actually see!

Activity
When you go on holiday, what are the kinds of things that you like to hear about when you sign up to a walking tour?

CHAPTER 28: FIVE SENSES

Our senses are often forgotten on a walking tour but can have a huge impact on the experience of your guests.

When you incorporate the senses into your tour, this often becomes the highlight for your guests. It is also a lot of fun to come up with different ideas to include the senses in the experience. Your goal is to enlighten and excite all the senses.

Here are some examples:

Sound

In a town, the sounds are the heartbeat of the community – children laughing, car doors slamming, supermarket trolleys clattering. If you are outside, are there birds you can point out? Or that train in the distance? Traffic? Or even the sound that the traffic light makes to indicate the light is green.

In the mid-1990s I did a 'Beatles' tour in London's West End. The guide brought along some Beatles music to play at relevant stops. It really made such a difference to the experience.

In the Blue Grotto on the Isle of Capri (Italy), we had gone into the cave in small boats of about four people with a guide. The experience was amazing! The colour of the water, the reflection of the light across the cave walls, it was truly incredible. And it will always be something I will talk about as a highlight of my travels, but what made it so special was that the guide started to sing. We were the only boat in the grotto, and his voice reverberated around us. It danced across the water. It enveloped us. It was truly magical! That was because he had tapped into the sense of sound, which elevated the experience.

Smell

If you are doing tours outside think about how you can encourage people to smell roses, or to notice the smell of freshly baked bread from the local bakery? Markets are full of wonderful smells – but make sure you point them out. Smell is an incredibly powerful sense.

I can still smell the cheese being made at a dairy farm in the Netherlands. It was horrible, but I will never forget the experience, because of it.

Touch

The simple touch of the stone of the church building, a statue, or wrought iron fencing can give your guests a real sense history. There are so many examples of touching statues for good luck.

In Verona, Italy, touching the breast of the statue of Juliet (of Shakespeare's 'Romeo and Juliet') is a good luck symbol of fertility.

Sight

Seeing is not just about pointing things out, but about consciously drawing your guests' attention to something. You might want to take them to a high point to get a better view.

The view from the Sky Tower in Auckland, New Zealand, gives a fantastic view of the city and a clear picture of the layout.

On walks I do in the City of London I have a folder of old photographs which I can show my guests to compare the modern city with the old historic images. It really does make things so much clearer.

Taste

This is an opportunity to introduce your guests to a local dish, or a region-specific pastry or drink. Maybe your region is well-known for cider or cheese, so it could be an idea to end the tour at a local pub or a food shop so that the guest can taste some local cuisine.

When I was working on a cruise ship in Russia, we stopped in a village along the river. In small groups we went into the homes of the locals and enjoyed their cooking and baking (I will admit it was a tough one to pretend to enjoy a cold cabbage-based cake - which really is not my favourite). But it was a wonderful experience I will never forget.

Enhance the Experience

When you consider all the senses, you enhance the overall experience and bring the destination to life. And in some ways, it relaxes everyone. Your walking tour becomes a voyage of self-exploration, and your guests will start to appreciate more of what you are showing them.

Every walk can be a 'wonderland' for the senses. And remember, what you take for granted might be something really unusual for your guests.

Be playful with this. It really does highlight your passion, excitement, experience, knowledge, and your skill as a tour guide.

Activity

Focus on each of the senses. Identify how you can incorporate them into your walking tour. It could be a real challenge to work out how you are going to encompass all the senses but give it a go.

CHAPTER 29: COLOUR YOUR WALKS

Interesting and exciting language can add colour to your walks. There may be phrases you can adapt to add something special to your tour commentary.

Personification

When you give an inanimate object a human characteristic, it can be very effective to bring a concept or object 'alive'.

Example: *"This tree is over 200 years old. Imagine the stories it could tell!"*

Cause and Effect

This is about explaining the process of an action which then has an ongoing or unexpected effect. This can leave an impact on your guests and is always a great way to explain how things happen.

Example: *"When Mr X carved the road through the valley, it brought traders to the area and these small towns prospered."*

Similes and Metaphors

Concepts are much easier to understand when we make comparisons.

Example: *"The thieves snaked through the crowds picking pockets as they went."*

Emphasis

It can be easy to lose a sense of perspective without context or a picture. If you can use emphasis to explain ideas, your guests will get a clearer understanding.

Example: *"The Duke paid £50,000 in 1800 for the estate, which is over £1 million in today's money."*

Physical Aids
You can physically show what something looks / looked like using a folder of images or samples of a product. Clothing can be a fun addition too.
Example: "*This is what the street looked like after it was bombed.*"

Active & Colourful Verbs
Verbs give our sentences action. Colourful verbs can describe something and add a sense of theatre too. Passive verbs have much less of an effect.
Example: "*The traffic streamed through the streets like a colony of ants.*"

Leading and Open-Ended Questions
Your questions can engage your group and give them something to ponder, consider and discuss with fellow guests, or even when they get home. Leading questions encourage your guests to think about outcomes and solutions. Open-ended questions need more than a 'yes' or a 'no' for the answer.
Example: "*What will this field look like in 20 years' time if these plans go ahead?*"

Mystery
Mystery can add a sense of drama and maybe even an 'ah-ha' moment. It is a fun way to get your guests involved too.
Example: "*Why has no one ever seen the man who locks the churchyard gates?*"

Modern Comparisons
Stories can often be difficult to grasp as they may seem foreign and out of context. Try to use modern examples to explain situations and events:
Example: "*People were lonely when they were boarded up in their homes during the Plague, just like the Pandemic of 2020.*"

Activity

For every stop on your tour, think about ways to colour your speech using some of the above examples. You will not be learning your walking tours off by heart, but as you get more familiar with your content, these sentences and phrases will come naturally.

Even if the facts are interesting, the delivery can leave guests feeling bored and disconnected. The more colour, the better!

CHAPTER 30: STORYTELLING

A walking tour guide is a storyteller.
Storytelling can be used to:

- Bring facts to life
- Emphasise a point
- Share a local myth or legend

You have 'poetic licence' to enhance the experience. Use it as much as you can!

How to tell a good story:
- Bring your group in closer for 'theatre'.
- Create an atmosphere by setting the scene using time, place, and environment (such a weather), to 'paint a picture'.
- Use pace, tone, volume, pitch, and expression to create drama.
- Your hands, facial expressions and body movements can help to convey shapes, scenery, actions, and feelings.
- Different voices for different characters will add to your story.
- Involve your guests by asking questions.
- Use silence to build anticipation and to hold attention.
- Include the senses and colour for an overall experience.

How to construct a story:
- Have a strong beginning.
- Make the middle 'meaty' with action and adventure.

- Consider an ending with impact.
- Notice your guests' responses to your stories. Use their unconscious feedback to improve and adapt your stories for future walking tours.

Activity

- Take a personal story you have told many times and 'play' with it. See how you can add in each of the points above and try it out with someone who has never heard the story before. Watch them carefully for feedback and adapt it as necessary.
- Now do the same thing with a local legend, myth, or story that you could include in your walking tour commentary.

Does the story sound more interesting and entertaining when you have enhanced it with some storytelling techniques?

CHAPTER 31:
SAFE ENVIRONMENT

It is vital that you encourage the group to take responsibility for their own safety. There is only one of you, and many of them. Make sure to mention this before you even start on the walk.

Overall, safety is much easier when you are fully prepared. Pre-tour, check your route and adapt it if necessary.

A walking tour may not seem long enough to build a trusting relationship, but through positive and interesting communication, you can develop a rapport with a group. This raises the groups confidence in you, the guide. Of course, this makes for an enjoyable and safe experience both for you and for your group.

Overall, your aim is to keep the group safe, and for them to feel that you have their safety as a priority too. Be conscious of local laws and regulations, agreements with organisations (such as not walking on the grass), as well as environmental and sustainable concerns (picking fruit for example).

Sometimes this is pointing out the obvious and sometimes, the 'not so obvious'.

Activity

It is important to investigate Public Liability insurance for your walking tours. And if you are guiding for an organisation, remind them to put you on their insurance policies. You may also be required to complete a risk-assessment.

Please do not put this off.

Ensure you have a plan and procedures for all emergencies. This will include having your mobile phone fully charged, phone numbers for the local emergency services and if you are working with, or for, an organisation, make sure you have their contact and 'out of hours' emergency numbers.

CHAPTER 32:
CREATE YOUR WALKING TOUR

Your walking tours will evolve and adapt according to your personality. Here I have put together some simple steps and guidelines to help you get started. You do not have to use these – it is just a guide. But it is a good place to start as it will give you some structure and confidence to deliver a walking tour with ease, and something special that your guests will enjoy.

Having a structure like this should also help you remember all the facts and the stories you want to share, especially when you are starting out.

Preparing your Walking Tour
1. Select a theme for your walk.
2. Decide on the length of time the walk is for (build in time to walk between the sites)
3. Where are you going to start and finish?
4. Identify the route you will be walking.

Be mindful of a walk being too long. Less is more.

"The mind can take as much as the feet can stand."
Dan Wood (Tour Director)

Pre-Tour
- Welcome everyone warmly with a smile.
- Introduce yourself.
- Ask the group:
  - Where are you from?
  - How long are you in X?
  - Have you been here before?
- COLLECT THE MONEY (if this is relevant)

Beginning of your walking tour
- Overview of the town history / region / area
- How did it start?
- What was / is the main industry?
- Population
- What is /was it famous for?
- Famous people from the area / town

GIVE LATE JOINERS AN OPPORTUNITY TO JOIN THE GROUP BEFORE YOU GIVE THE MOST IMPORTANT HEALTH & SAFETY INFORMATION

Start
About the tour
Include aspects of the tour that will grab imagination of your participants. This could be a few facts that you can refer to later on, such as historical links with their home country, an unusual plant, a famous person, a specific artefact. And it will give them something to look forward to. Think of this as your 'teaser' - like a movie trailer.

Use this as an opportunity to slowly develop familiarity with a topic. This helps to build understanding.

- *Let the group know:*
  Where they are standing
  Where the tour will end
  Length of the tour
- *Health and safety & 'housekeeping' to mention:*
  To stay with the group.
  That you will be crossing the road as a group.
  The side of the road the cars drive on.
  To keep an eye out for bicycles.
  Location of the facilities.
  Breaks and opportunities along the route.

Advise the group to take their photographs along the way and then re-join the group.

Let them know that you will get to a stop and take a few minutes to wait for the group. Remind them that waiting too long will lengthen the tour for everyone.

Each Stop
- Top Visual Priority (TVP) What is the most obvious thing they can see?
- Where are they standing?
- What can they see around the group?
- Plan in your head:
  - Location
  - Architecture
  - History
  - People
  - Today
  - Legend / Story

Last Stop
- Tell them where they are
- How do they get back to the start? (If you are not finishing where you started)
- Where are the nearest facilities?
- What can they do after the tour?
- When is the next tour?
- Remind them to tell friends and family about the lovely tour they have been on
- Mention social media channels they can find you on
- Where can they find out more information? (Direct them to the Tourist Information Centre for example)
- Future and other themed tours available

Activity

Now it is time to put your walking tour together. Hoorah!

To reduce the stress and anxiety, focus on being fully prepared for your walking tour. Read around your subject and theme as much as you can and join walking tours with experienced guides so you can learn how they deliver their information and what kind of content they share. Also notice how they manage their guests.

Create a Rough Script

You will not be reading your walking tour notes and you also do not want to be over-rehearsed. But a rough script with a format, will give you some confidence. You may want to rehearse your introduction and your conclusion, but the rest of your walk needs to flow and be adapted to the environment, circumstances and to your guests.

Choose Your Props

Props can act as prompts to remind you about your content. It is such a creative and fun part of a walking tour. Find ways to bring props into your commentary to add colour and fun. Your guests will love it!

Consider how you are going to carry the props on your walk and how you will introduce them at the relevant place, physically and in your commentary.

Make Your Content Relatable

Find ways to make your content, stories, and facts, relevant and relatable to your group's lives. Therefore, you want to ask at the beginning of the walk, where they are from. This can help you draw comparisons and give the walk a more personal angle. And your group will understand and remember what you share with them.

Practise, Practise, Practise!

Find friends and colleagues to take out on your walking tours to vary and adapt your stories, and to test your material. This will help you practise your timings and iron out any glitches. You will feel so much more comfortable when you take your first group out on your new walking tour.

Most importantly: have fun!

Section 6: Questions & Answers

CHAPTER 33: BETWEEN STOPS

"I had a walking safari two days ago. There is quite a distance from one point to another. What should I do with the group between the stops?"
Roger - Driver / Guide in Tanzania, East Africa

Suggestions
When you move from stop to stop you could keep your group engaged:
1. Give them things to *look out for* along the way. Make sure you have spoken about these things before or after they have seen them.
2. Give your guests something to *think about* so that when you come together, you can get them engaged with the conversation.

You do not need to fill every second of your walk with information or activities. Your group will also need time to digest the information you have shared with them and enjoy what they are looking at.

The time between stops is a chance for you to mentally prepare for your next stop by going over the information in your head. If you need this time and you suspect your group will use the walks between stops as an opportunity to chat to you and ask you questions, make sure you give them something to look out for or think about. This will give you time and space to get ready for your next stop.

Activity

Don't forget to build in time for the group to explore on their own too. This could be after your walk, to keep the pace of your tour solid but leisurely.

CHAPTER 34: DRYING UP

"I am so worried I will be prepared for my walking tour and then on the day, I will be so nervous, I will dry up. What can I do?"
Chris – local walking tour guide in Somerset, UK

Did you know the thing people fear the most is public speaking? Yes, people are more scared of speaking publicly, than even dying. I am not sure what aspect of public speaking frightens people. It could be a fear of drying up, and not having anything more to say. We create these scenarios in our minds - a room full of people waiting for us to say something, and there is nothing there.

Our brains are not able to spit anything out.

As a guide, you **WILL** dry up, especially when you first start guiding.

Suggestion
You do not need to tell everything you know. Less is more.

If you 'dry up' between stops, you could also tell your group what they could look out for on the next stretch. Then let them just walk, observing the world around them, listening to the birds, or looking out for what you told them to spot.

That gives them time to absorb what you have shared, and it gives you an opportunity to prepare for your next stop.

What can you do, if suddenly, you have nothing more to say?

The best advice is to ***pause.***

The pause will give your group time to contemplate what you have said, and absorb the content in relation to what is around them.

Do not ever think of theses pauses as negatives, but rather as opportunities for your group and for you to gather your thoughts.

To give you additional confidence, (especially if you are nervous), is to learn the opening lines of your commentary for each stop on your walking tour.

For example, if there are 12 stops on your walking tour, have 12 lines in your head, which you have learned by rote. Even if you just remember these 12 lines, it is enough. And, if you remember more, that's great. If not, you just need to get that one line out as a minimum at each stop.

Then, have a look at what you can see around you. This might trigger something additional. If not, you have given your group something (no matter how little you feel it is), before you move on to the next stop. As you gain more experience, your content will flow naturally, but until then this one-line technique is something to fall back on.

Remember, you never need to apologise for drying up.

Most of the people in your group will not even notice that there is a break in the commentary.

As soon as you feel you are 'drying up', pause, and say, "Shall we move on?" That gives you time while you are walking from one place to another, to gather your thoughts.

This does not always work. People will try to catch up with you in those walking periods to ask question. But, it is a technique that you can try because your group will never notice that you have paused, unless you draw their attention to it. If you say, "Oh no! I don't know! I have forgotten what I was going to say!" you are more likely to panic. When you panic, the group will notice that you have 'dried up'.

Pauses are really positive because you know you are going to give them a lot of information during their walking tour, so a little pause is a good thing.

If you dry up because of nervousness:

- Stand confidently. You will feel good and in command of your knowledge.
- Smile! Even if you are nervous, nobody will know if you smile. This generally softens everything about your body and your breathing.
- Establish eye contact. This connects you with people, and human connection will help you relax.
- Use meaningful gestures.
- Practice correct breathing to help all of the above points.

CHAPTER 35: COMMON MISTAKES

"I am starting out. What are some of the common mistakes guides make, that I can avoid, or at least try to?"
Clive – city walking tour guide in Johannesburg, South Africa

When you are aware of some of the most common mistakes walking tour guides make, you can ensure you do not make them yourself:

Human Encyclopaedia Guide
If people in your group want an historic or fact-heavy lecture, they would not come on a walking tour. Use facts, figures, and complicated concepts only if your group has specialist knowledge. A Latin name is interesting only if you use it to explain why and how things happen or link the name of something to it. Fun facts, stories, interesting snippets, and 'wow' facts will keep your group engaged. As soon as you see them glaze over, you know you are boring them.

Keep is simple, short and avoid jargon and technical words and details.

Know-It-All Guide
No one likes a 'know it all'. Even if you are the expert, and you know more about the town or the region than your group, be humble with your knowledge. Do not feel the urge to correct your guests or presume you know more than they do. There is an arrogance that comes with someone who thinks they know everything. If you continue to learn, train, read and engage with new and fresh content, you will grow as a guide and inspire your guests.

The Ferris Wheel Guide
There are guides who do the same walking tour repeatedly.

They share the same facts, tell the same stories, and follow the same route. This must bore them eventually. And if it bores them, it will bore their guests too.

Even if your walk is on the same route, find some fresh content, fun facts, and new stories. You could even change the theme of the walk, even though it follows the same route.

Mix it up a bit to keep it fresh.

Fictional Storyteller Guide

Making up stories might sound fun, but if you get caught out, you may be a little embarrassed. If you do have a fictional story that you want to use, you could say something like:

"Apparently this is true...." or "There are some that believe...." or "There is a story I heard, but I don't know how true it is."

That way you are covered, and you can embellish the facts a little, but you have made it clear that it may not be true.

Scripted Guide

Never learn your walking tour off-by-heart. When you get nervous, you will forget your lines. This leads to panic and can have an awful effect on your walking tour.

The best technique is to learn your information in chunks. Each chunk is a new heading, and you can gather all your information under that heading. All you need to learn is the chunks. Share what you know from that chunk and move onto the next one.

Let your content flow. Make is conversational and chatty. Keep it informal and fun!

Wishful Thinking Guide

If there is a need during the walking tour for your guests to pay an entrance fee for something else, collect the money up-front before the start of the tour. When you use your own money (in the hope of collecting the fee from your guests later), you will find that you end up losing out. Your visitors can get so involved in the experience that they forget to pay you.

CHAPTER 36:
WHEN PEOPLE LEAVE

"Sometimes on my walking tour, people just leave without saying goodbye. They just disappear. How can I avoid it?"
Antonia – city guide in Edinburgh, Scotland, UK

People may leave your tour for several reasons, and it is probably not because of you. They could be tired or cold, have theatre tickets, a train to catch or the walk is not what they thought it would be about.

Suggestions
If you tell the group exactly what to expect at the beginning of your walk, they can make their mind up before you start.
It might just not be for them.
You could also mention at the beginning of the walk, that if anyone does want to leave the walk at any time, to please give you a wave and come and say goodbye. Remind them, that when you get to the next stop, you may wait for them. So, it would be good if they could tell you that they are leaving, or you may worry they are lost. This is also not fair on your other guests.

Rather focus on those who are there and who are interested, even if it is just one other person.

If you are doing a paid walk and you need to collect money, people may disappear to avoid paying you at the end. Consider collecting the money up-front, to save the frustration and embarrassment.

CHAPTER 37: MEETING YOUR GUESTS

"Do you have any recommendations for when I first meet the guests for my walking tour? When they are nervous and awkward, I feel nervous and awkward."
Angela – garden guide in Cumbria, UK

People can be very shy when they arrive on your walking tour. They will often stand far away from you and sometimes from the others on the walking tour.

You can 'break the ice' and make them feel part of the group by trying these simple tips:

Introduce Yourself
Sometimes people are not sure they are in the right place. They may have been given a name of the guide and they have no way of knowing that you are their guide. If you are warm and friendly, right from the start, your guests will know they are with the right guide and they will relax a little.

Ask Questions
Ask your guests questions to put them at ease, almost immediately. It is so much easier for people to talk about themselves. They may then engage with others in the group, and they may even find some common ground between them.

Reassurance
If your guests are unfamiliar with the town, area, or region where you are guiding, they may be concerned about getting back to where they know their car is, or the coach is picking them up from (for example). They may also be concerned that the walking tour will over-run and they could miss their train or their next engagement. Often guests may not want to stop to take any photographs in case you continue without them, and

they may get lost. Keep your group informed of times and places they can stop for the facilities, photographs, shopping etc.

Always be clear where you will meet them at the next stop. Give them reassurance from the beginning and for the duration of your walking tour.

Enthusiasm

Be enthusiastic! You are of course passionate about where you are guiding, so show your guests your love for life, knowledge, and stories. Enthusiasm is contagious and your group will have the best time!

CHAPTER 38:
WHAT QUESTIONS TELL US

"I wish people wouldn't ask so many questions on my walking tours!"
Gerry – Uluru guide, Australia

When your guests ask you questions, you can deduce:

- Your group is listening, is interested, and engaged with your content.
- They have a specific interest – which is a clue to what might interest them further along the walking tour.
- They are comfortable asking you questions because they feel that you are approachable and welcoming.
- The information you are giving out is relevant to the group.
- The group is enjoying your tour.

When someone is brave enough to ask a question, you should be thankful, grateful and give them the answer they deserve.

Questions are a golden opportunity. They are clues to what you can incorporate into your future tours with additional research.

Be mindful and listen carefully to the questions your group asks and make the most of them.

Section 7: Professional Tips

CHAPTER 39: TOOLS OF THE TRADE

1. Props

A great way to enhance your walking tour is to include props, accessories or clothing that is relevant to your theme. You could also have a folder with images to show how things have changed, or to explain concepts and processes.

Props and images are helpful for those who are hard of hearing, or who do not speak your language fluently. They will get a much clearer picture of what you are talking about and will feel part of the group and the experience.

2. Microphones / Headphones

Make sure you test all equipment before the walking tour starts. If batteries are needed, make sure you carry spare batteries to avoid problems.

If you have a clip-on microphone, work out the best place to attach it to your clothing. Scarves, beards, jewellery, lanyards etc can rub against it, which can make a very unpleasant sound. Having your mouth too close to the microphone can distort your voice, and turning your head could mean your guests lose half your sentence.

And do not forget to switch your microphone off (or unplug it completely) when you are not talking to your group. It could cause embarrassment for you and your guests.

3. Pointer / Laser

Sometimes it is impossible to explain where you want your group to look. There may be some intricate architecture you want to point out, or a specific aspect of a large painting hanging high up in a stairwell of the gallery. A laser pointer is a great tool to consider for situations like these.

4. Comfortable shoes

There are few things that make a guide's life easier than a pair of comfortable shoes. Be sure that you can cover the terrain with ease (cobbled paths, muddy landscape etc). Be smart, but your priority should be shoes that allow you to function without distraction.

5. Bottle of water

When you talk a lot, as you will when you are guiding, you will need to hydrate your throat. It is a simple item to remember to take on your walking tours but has a huge impact on how you are able to perform in your role.

6. First Aid Kit

When you are doing short walking tours in a town, a first aid kit is not important. You are around people, and you have mobile phone signal. But if your walking tour is out in the bush, or in the countryside, where there are few people or you may not have mobile phone signal, it is worth considering a small first aid kit for simple things like band aids for blisters, safety pins for a broken shoe etc. You are not legally allowed to dispense medication (for in or on the body) unless you have relevant certification.

If you are guiding for an organisation, know and understand their regulations and procedures. If you are working for yourself, ensure that you are covered with insurance, know what support is available and have your own emergency procedures.

CHAPTER 40: BODIES AND ORGANISATIONS

In some countries, such as Greece, Spain and Italy**, it is against the law to guide without a professional, accredited guiding qualification from their officially recognised body. Once you have qualified as a guide, you will also be invited to join the guiding communities where you will make connections, get support, training, resources, professional development, and updates about the profession.

**There are opportunities in these countries to become 'orientation or welcome' guides. These are company representatives who are not allowed to guide (share historic knowledge, for example) but can orientate their guests with maps and ideas about things to do and places to visit.

If you are in a country where you can guide without official accreditation, you may consider doing some training under the official guiding umbrella organisations.

The Institute of Tourist Guiding, in the UK, is:

"a professional membership organisation which is committed to developing, maintaining and promoting professional standards in tourist guiding."

Once you have passed an Institute of Tourist Guiding accredited course, you will be able to join the membership community with all the benefits that comes with being a trained and accredited tourist guide.

In the United Kingdom, there are currently three levels of further guide training:

White Badge
This badge is for those who wish to volunteer to guide in museums, historic buildings such as stately homes, art galleries, theme parks and other attractions.

Green Badge
This badge covers those interested in doing paid guiding (employed or self-employed) at visitor attractions and on walking tours in smaller areas such as in a town, site of interest or a garden.

Blue Badge
This is the highest level of guiding qualification in the United Kingdom. The training is for a much larger region and metropolitan area and includes walking tours and guiding on other forms of transport, such as coaches.

Insurance
It is important to protect yourself and your guests by getting yourself insured. Anything can happen on your walking tour that could be out of your control, but it is your responsibility to yourself and your guests to ensure you are all safe.

If you are guiding for an organisation, make sure they have included you on their insurance policy. This is something they often forget to do, so keep reminding them until you are fully covered.

Continued Professional Development (CPD)

To continue to be an engaging and interesting guide, you need to grow professionally and keep yourself up to date and informed.

Besides official tourist guiding bodies, there are organisations and community groups you can join, or visit, to keep learning and to raise your own profile locally:

- **Local history groups**

You will learn so much more about your local area / town, and you could also offer to do talks which the members will enjoy. You will expand your knowledge as you will need to do research for the talk. And you will raise your own profile as the local walking tour guide.

- **Women's Institute (WI)**

If you are in the UK, Canada, South Africa and New Zealand, there are many opportunities to audition to be an official speaker at WI events across the country. This too will help you grow your confidence, knowledge and raise your profile.

- **Business Networking Groups**

If you are charging for your walking tours, you are in effect a small business. You will be amazed at how many contacts you can make at local business networking events. Other business owners could become your allies (restaurants, shops, pubs) or your customers / guest on your walking tours. And of course, they too have a wide network. Their network could become aware of you once you engage with them.

- **Chambers of Commerce**

Local and regional Chambers of Commerce work closely with tourism organisations to increase visitors to the area, who will of course spend money. Raise your profile and make new contacts by joining and / or attending local, regional, and county Chamber events.

- **Town Council**

Every town council has a mandate to grow their income by attracting visitors from the outside. Connect with your local counsellor and / or the person at the local town council who is responsible for tourism or supporting small businesses in the area. They will want to support you, and may even employ you to run regular walking tours in your town, village, or area.

- **Museums and Art Galleries**

Your local museums and art galleries are great sources of information for your walking tour research, and can provide opportunities for you to speak at events, head up projects and engage the community. Make friends with these organisations. Let them know that you are doing walking tours locally. You never know what these relationships could open up for you.

All engagements are opportunities for growth.

Activity

- Research all your local opportunities to raise your profile, expand your knowledge and increase your network.
- Reach out to as many people, bodies, and organisations as possible, to let them know who you are, what walking tours you are doing and how you can collaborate with them.

CHAPTER 41: TALKING TO THE PUBLIC

How do you tell the public about your walking tours?

It is important to consider what marketing and promotion you are going to do to reach people so that you can let them know they can come and enjoy your walking tour/s. You may be doing these walks as free experiences, or you may be charging for your walks. Either way, you need to get the word out about your brilliant walking tours.

Marketing & Public Relations

- **Tourist Information, Museums & Art Galleries**

Contact your local tourist information, museum/s and art galleries as soon as you are considering your walking tours. They may have an opportunity for you to join their team. Maybe you are the first guide to approach them, so you could get involved in something new from the start. There may already be routes and themes of walks created and you could slot into those. You may be very surprised at what is available and on offer, and this could be the most valuable connection you make.

- **Facebook Business Page**

It is not professional, or wise to use your Facebook personal profile to promote your walking tours.

You want to attract more people and if you are just sharing your content to your friends and family, even as a public post, you are limiting your reach.

You can only have a maximum of 5,000 friends, but a Business Page has no limits.

And of course, if you are marketing something, you want to see the statistics such as reach, engagement, likes and shares. A Business Page will give you an in-depth analysis of your content so you can do more of what works and less of what doesn't.

Consider that there are almost 3 billion people on Facebook, so you have a very large potential audience. Even if you are guiding locally, and do not need to reach millions, these numbers are an indication of how many people locally will be on Facebook, in local Facebook groups and interested in your walking tours.

- **Instagram**

If you enjoy taking photographs on your smartphone and love the creativity of this artform, Instagram is a brilliant platform to share your content. Once you master the hashtags and the simplicity of this 'less noisy' platform, you will start reaching your target audience in no time.

A business account (which is free), will also give you the relevant statistics such as reach and engagement. This helps you craft your future posts accordingly.

- **LinkedIn**

LinkedIn is a business platform. It is not the place to promote your walking tours, but it is the place to show your expertise and connect with other professionals. You could find collaboration and training opportunities and you can join professional groups where you can find additional support.

- **Twitter**

Twitter is the best platform for instant and concise messaging. Many local communities use Twitter very effectively to share current information. If your target audience is on Twitter, consider how you can reach them using the effective and local hashtags. Make sure to follow the relevant local influencers, community organisations as well as those who are your walking tour allies (restaurants, pubs, tourist sites etc)

- **YouTube**

YouTube is owned by Google and is also the second largest search engine after its owner. It is one of the first places people go to find information and if you have a smartphone, you can record film that will attract potential guests. You do not need to be on camera yourself. You can point the camera away from yourself and talk about what you are showing. You can get more involved in the tech if you want to learn to put 'bells and whistles' on your content, but just you talking while walking, is a great way to 'tease' your potential audience.

- **TikTok**

If you enjoy fun, creative video, TikTok is for you. You can grow a following quite quickly when you upload short videos of where you are guiding, your area of expertise and fun facts to whet the appetite of your potential visitors.

- **Local Newspaper**

You can pay for a small advertisement in your local newspaper for your scheduled walking tours, or you could promote yourself as a local guide who is available to do walking tours for community groups, families, tourist groups etc.

Why not offer to do a regular column in the local paper? This is an opportunity to showcasing your knowledge, share snippets of information and 'teasers' for your walking tours and to engage the community in your walking tour themes.

- **Email List**

It is interesting to note that people are more likely to engage with email than with social media posts. The social media platforms choose who sees your posts, but if you send an email out to your subscribers, they will all receive the email, and they can open it when they choose. They are more likely to see your content.

It is great fun to send out regular emails with interesting information and fun facts about your area of guiding. And people are more likely to remember when you have your next walk, if they have read it on an email, rather than seen it fleeting past in their social media news feed.

You can sign up to a range of free email providers, so investigate the best one to suit your needs.

- **Local Radio**

Community radio stations are always looking for content. You could either be a regular guest on programmes about local activities, or you could have your own show. It is great fun to join a new community and a lot more opportunities will arise.

- **Blogging**

You do not need to be a 'writer' or a 'blogger' to write regular blogs. You can host them on your own website (which can be really reasonable to host) and you can learn to build your website quite easily. It is not as difficult as you think. You can share short pieces of interest and promote the dates and times of your next walking tours.

It is possible to attract a brand-new audience by offering to guest blogs on other websites. Reach out to websites / blogs that align with your theme and knowledge and offer to write a guest blog for them (maybe even a series of blog posts, or a regular contribution). They love content which they do not have to create, and you get to expand your reach with their audience.

- **Posters and Flyers**

Talk to people locally, to find out where the best places are to put up posters. Your local council may also have some boards in public areas, so find out from them. Cafes, restaurants, and supermarkets may also have local notice boards. And of course, hotels, Bed and Breakfast accommodation and guest houses, are another great source for promotion.

- **Travel Companies**

Are there travel / coach companies that come through your area? Contact them to let them know what you are doing and ask if there is anything they need locally. They may ask you to do a walking tour for their guests, even if they are just passing through. Being their direct contact in the area could also open other opportunities.

Promotional Tips

1. Update all your social media profiles with 'Walking Tour Guide in xx'
2. Create some business cards so you can hand them out at local events, business networking or at social events.
3. Do not use social media only as a sales tool. Share fun historical facts, information about you, behind the scenes, and general interest that your audience will enjoy.
4. Always get permission from your guests if you are going to use images of them on your promotion and social media channels.
5. Be creative! Find new and creative ways to let people know about your walking tours.
6. Keep a diary of your walks. Record incidents, good and bad. These will help you grow, but also provides you with some content for your marketing.

Customer Service

Consider how your customer is contacting you and what their experience is? Ask yourself:

1. Was it easy for them to connect with me?
2. Is the process to book onto my walking tours simple?
3. Do my potential customers have all their questions answered? (Where could they find the information if not?)
4. If the walking tour is cancelled, how can I let my guests know?

From the moment your audience connects with you, you take them on a customer service journey. Assess each point of service to make sure you do not lose them because the process is complicated or difficult.

Some points to think about:

1. Do you have an email address available online for the public to use? (If not, create one just for your guiding).
2. Do you have a phone number that is accessible for the public to use? (You may want to consider a 'pay as you go' option that is separate from your personal phone).
3. Does your social media messaging have auto-response messages set up to let people know that you will be in touch, or another way they can contact you if there is an urgent need?
4. Have you put a system in place to connect with your past guests? You may ask for their email address during the payment process. Make sure you have the relevant requests for their details in line with date protection legalities.
5. How will your customers know when to meet, what to bring and wear etc? This will depend on the marketing you have done (the information may be on a flyer or in a Facebook event for example). Or if they have booked online, you may have their email address so you can share this type of information before the walking tour.

This may all seem overwhelming, but remember, you do not need to do everything. Start with getting your walk up and running, take friends and family out to raise your confidence and then consider how you are going to take the next step. Each of the ideas given will be enough on their own. But it also depends on what your plans and goals are for your walking tours and what you know, are interested to learn more about and also what you enjoy doing already.

Activity

Answer these questions from Chapter 2 (What is a Walking Tour?) again:

- What do visitors expect of a good tour guide?
- What are the key roles and responsibilities of an effective tour guide?
- What preparations are needed before taking out a walking tour?
- How does a tour guide handle questions (especially from difficult guests)?
- What are the qualities of a good tour guide?

Compare your answers.

Now that you have more knowledge, you may surprise yourself with your answers.

CHAPTER 42: FROM THE PROFESSIONALS

Sandy Barker

Sandy Barker is a Best-Selling Australian author. She ran coach tours in Europe and as part of those tours, she would conduct walking tours.

Top Tip: Tell the Story

"It's great to have those fun facts, the dates and figures all correct, but you really want to tell the story to bring it to life."

Dan Wood

Dan Wood has run coach tours all over the United Kingdom in Ireland for the last 30 years. During that time, he has taken out many walking tours.

Tip 1: Explaining History

"Make history as much fun as possible. People aren't on your walking tour to get a degree in the subject. They are there to be entertained. You can always fracture your history with examples of using modern technology, like mobile phones and texting. It's amazing how many laughs you get when you hear that Henry VIII 'texted' his Chancellor, to say: Chop her head off!"

Tip 2: Use Location Wisely

"York is one of my favourite places to lead a walking tour. It can often be damp and windy. If you stand your groups in front of the west door of the Minster, which is arched and has steps leading up to it, it serves two purposes:

1. To keep your people out of the rain.
2. The arch itself acts like a sound box. You can project your voice over wind and rain. At the same time your group also get something great to look at. No, not you!

Walking Tour Guiding

The archway over the door of the west front of the magnificent York Minster."

Tony Jenkins

Tony Jenkins is a Welsh cruise director working on riverboats mostly in France. From time to time, he has been a local tour guide as well.

Tip 1: Where are your guests from?

"It is very important to ascertain what nationalities you're dealing with. You can then cater for such things as Celsius and Fahrenheit to ensure that you know how hot somewhere is or cold somewhere is in the winter."

Tip 2: Mobility Issues

"It is important to know if you have any mobility issues in your group. You don't want to walk too fast. You may have people who are much slower, and they paid the same price as everybody else.

Tip 3: Make your guests feel special

"You should always make eye contact with the guests, which is also important to make them feel comfortable. You want them to know you are engaging with them personally, and they hopefully they'll have a great experience."

Tip 4: Knowledge as story

"I think knowledge is very, very important. But sometimes people get bogged down with statistics and dates, and these are things that the people will probably not remember. However, if you tell them a little story or an anecdote about the town, these are things they will remember."

Mark Carter

Mark Carter is a trainer, speaker, writer, and director of the Mark Carter Learning Academy. In a former life Mark was a tour leader with Contiki Holidays and for the Travel Corporation. He was also a training manager for four years, developing leaders, and teaching walking tours, was a component of that role.

Tip 1: Keep Expanding Your Knowledge

"Do not rest on your laurels. It's probably even more important in this day and age because the speed and pace of information that people get access to. Keep reading, keep learning, and keep looking for points of interest to keep it fresh. It's a great way to make sure that you're always on point."

Tip 2: Pace of the walking tour

"I know people have different ideas around this. Mine would be ultimately that you need to set the pace. You're setting the itinerary, you're setting a schedule. If you leave it in other people's hands, you're going to slow it down and may never get it done. So, be mindful that people may walk slower than you, but set a pace. And make sure you find mechanisms to keep people on track with that. You don't want your guests to miss out and you want them to complete the walking tour comfortably."

Tip 3: Balance stories, knowledge, and self-discovery

"Make sure you've built in plenty of time for a nice mix while walking between points of interest, great knowledge and stories to bring it all to life. And you need to have some time for self-discovery. But be really clear with your directions and timings, so that your group can meet you again after they have explored."

CHAPTER 43: THAT'S A WRAP

And that's it!

But this is, of course, only just the beginning. You now have some skills that you can use to create and lead walking tours locally, or you may want to explore opportunities abroad or lead groups internationally.

Ultimately, this is the foundation of great things to come. I hope that I have been able to inspire you to raise your confidence and the skills for you to take further.

Walking tour guiding is hugely enjoyable and always produces such an incredible buzz!

Now go out there and make magic, fulfil dreams and be amazing!

Activity

Remember those goals you wrote down in Chapter 1?
- Why do you want to lead walking tours?
- What do you hope to achieve as a walking tour guide?
- Where would you like to guide?
- Do you have different walking tours in mind?

Do not let these goals disappear - revisit them and amend them as needed to remain inspired.

I really feel so privileged to have been a part of your guiding journey and I look forward to hearing where your path takes you and how your guiding journey progresses.

If you have any more questions, please get in touch with me: dawn@dawnadenton.com

I would love to hear all your guiding stories!

Best wishes always,

Dawn (https://dawnadenton.com/)

ABOUT THE AUTHOR

Dawn A Denton describes herself as a 'multipotentialite'. She lives in Frome, Somerset, UK with her other half and their gorgeous dog Doris, in an 18th century house, which of course, has many stories to tell.
Dawn is a member of the Frome Writers Collective, teaches content creation, is a trainer, public speaker and supports her Southern African community abroad.

For more information, opportunities, and tips, scan this QR code or visit:

https://dawnadenton.com/walkingtourguidingbook/

www.ingramcontent.com/pod-product-compliance
Lightning Source LLC
Chambersburg PA
CBHW032049090426
42744CB00004B/133